BULGARIA

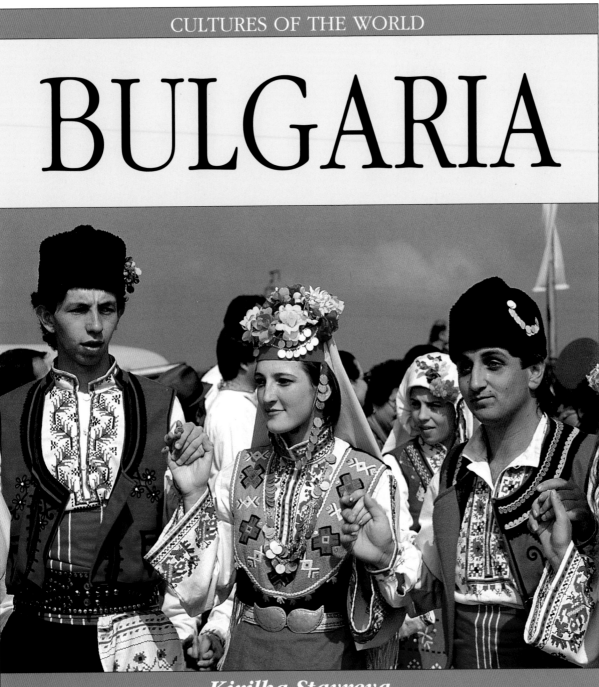

Kirilka Stavreva

MARSHALL CAVENDISH
New York • London • Sydney

Reference Edition published 1997 by
Marshall Cavendish Corporation
99 White Plains Road
Tarrytown
New York 10591

© Times Editions Pte Ltd 1997

Originated and designed by
Times Books International, an imprint of
Times Editions Pte Ltd

Printed in Singapore

Library of Congress Cataloging-in-Publication Data:
Stavreva, Kirilka.
    Bulgaria / Kirilka Stavreva.
        p.   cm. — (Cultures of the world)
    Includes bibliographical references and index.
    Summary: Describes the geography, history, government,
economy, and culture of this country in the heart of the
Balkan peninsula.
    ISBN 0-7614-0286-1 (lib. bdg.)
    1. Bulgaria—Juvenile literature. [1. Bulgaria.] I. Title.
II. Series.
DR55.S76   1997
949.77—dc20   96–21342
                                                CIP
                                                AC

Pub. 10/96   21.00L

INTRODUCTION

BULGARIA IS A COUNTRY still undiscovered by the world. Except for the rare upset of some world power in soccer, it has hardly ever made international headlines. The few who can put Bulgaria on the map recognize it as a Communist ally of the collapsed Soviet Union, but see it as an obscure place somewhere in the turbulent Balkans between Europe and Asia.

There is much more to Bulgaria than its recent Communist past. It is a stronghold of Slavic culture and a peaceful haven in the war-torn Balkans. It is also a land of mythical beauty, with a long and dramatic history. Its people are industrious and courageous, with many literary and artistic achievements to their name. Above all, the country is now undergoing profound and painful changes in the economic, political, and cultural arenas.

CONTENTS

Bulgarian mother and child.

CONTENTS

Winter in Plovdiv.

GEOGRAPHY

BULGARIA IS IN THE HEART of the Balkan peninsula, in southeastern Europe. The country has an eastern coast washed by the Black Sea, giving it strategic access to both the Sea of Marmara and the Mediterranean Sea. Its southern neighbors are Turkey and Greece.

To the west lie Macedonia and Yugoslavia. In the north, the river Danube separates it from Romania. The total land area of Bulgaria is 42,823 square miles (110,912 square km), making it only slightly larger than Tennessee in the United States.

For such a small country, Bulgaria's natural terrain is strikingly varied. There are majestic mountains cut by deep gorges, fertile plains and lowlands, and a dramatic sea coast. No single feature dominates the landscape, which may change with every turn of the road.

The Balkan range of mountains divides the country into the two parts of north and south, with the Black Sea coast forming a third region.

Opposite: **The pine-covered slopes of Pirin attract hikers from all over Europe.**

Below: **The Bulgarian Black Sea coast presents a striking relief of steep cliffs alternating with long sandy beaches.**

A PARADISE ON EARTH

How Bulgaria became a country of such variety and beauty is explained in an old legend.

It seems that the Bulgarian was busy cultivating his garden on the day that God was giving out land to the various nations. When the man finally made it to heaven, all the land had already been parceled out. "You won't leave me without a country, will you?" implored the Bulgarian.

God thought for a moment, and then smiled broadly, "I have the solution for you. Since all the world has been already divided up, I will give your people a piece of paradise."

Sunflowers flourish in northern Bulgaria, an area rich in the production of grains and oilseeds.

THREE DISTINCT REGIONS

The Balkan range divides the country into two parts. There is the fertile Danubian plain in the north, and in the south is the region of high mountains, enclosed valleys, and the large Thracian plain. The third distinct area is the Black Sea coast.

Northern Bulgaria has been the country's golden granary since the seventh century, when the Slav and Bulgar tribes united to form the beginnings of Bulgaria. In recent times, a prosperous food and beverage industry has developed in the region, based on the production of grains and oilseeds.

Veliko Turnovo, or Turnovo for short, is one of Bulgaria's oldest cities, and overlooks the winding Yantra river. Its fortress stone walls testify to its importance as the medieval capital. But in modern-day Turnovo, heavy industry takes equal place with historical monuments such as churches and castles.

In southern Bulgaria warm Mediterranean air reaches the region along the river valleys, and the Balkan range acts as a climatic barrier against cold northern influences. These weather conditions, along with fertile soils and abundant mountain waters, favor the growing of vegetables, fruits, grapevines and cotton. The Bulgarian oil-bearing rose, the only descendant of the Persian rose surviving in Europe, also thrives here.

Bulgaria is blessed with abundant mountain pastures and fertile land.

Most of the big cities in southern Bulgaria, including the capital Sofia, are encircled by prosperous farms. Light industry, including tobacco processing and textiles, is well represented in this region. So is heavy industry, such as nonferrous metallurgy, machine building, chemicals, timber processing, and cement production.

The highest mountains in the Balkan peninsula rise in the southwest of Bulgaria. The rugged profiles of the Rila and Pirin ranges attract hikers and skiers from all over Europe, and the gently rolling slopes of the Rhodope range provide excellent conditions for winter tourism. Vast mountain pastures encourage cattle breeding and the raising of sheep.

The eastern parts of the Rhodope are inhabited mainly by Bulgarian Turks, who make good use of the favorable soils and sunny, arid climate to cultivate top-grade Oriental tobacco.

Cheese and yogurt are produced from sheep raised in southern Bulgaria.

BLACK SEA COAST

The country's eastern boundary is approximately 154 miles (248 km) long. This is the Black Sea coast, where steep cliffs with underwater caves alternate with long sandy beaches, and jungle-like vegetation grows along the mouths of rivers. Small, picturesque fishing towns stand side by side with large industrial port cities. The petrochemical, shipbuilding, metal processing, and electrical appliance industries are well-developed in this region. Raw materials are imported, but finished products are exported to numerous other countries.

THE HOMELAND OF YOGURT

Yogurt is a staple of the Bulgarian diet. It can be eaten plain, or made into a drink, salad dressing, or cold soup. Bulgarian yogurt is usually made from cow's milk, but sheep's or goat's milk can also be used. Yogurt from sheep's milk is considered a delicacy.

The bacteria responsible for the fermentation of Bulgarian yogurt has a very unstable life outside of the country. Apart from being a rich source of calcium, Bulgarians also believe that their yogurt contributes to their longevity.

FOUR SEASONS

Bulgaria has a temperate continental climate. However, the weather is conditioned by diverse elements such as the humid cyclones of the North Atlantic, the severe anticyclones of the Siberian plain, and mild air currents that come from the Mediterranean Sea.

The average annual temperatures are about 51° F (11° C) for northern Bulgaria and 56° F (13° C) for southern Bulgaria. The coldest winter month is January, when temperatures average 23° F (−5° C) in the north, and up to 36° F (2° C) in the south.

It is much colder in the mountains, while winters on the Black Sea coast are mild, with temperatures averaging around 36° F (2° C).

HOT SUMMERS

Summers are hot but tolerable. July is the hottest month for the whole country, with temperatures between 70 and 75° F (21 and 24° C), although it is cooler in the high mountains.

A village in the mountains can be very cold in winter.

Rain is the most common precipitation, but there are heavy winter snowfalls over the northern plains and the mountains. Precipitation is evenly distributed across the country and throughout the four seasons.

Because of the diverse terrain, there are no tornadoes, hurricanes, sandstorms, or other strong winds of this nature. The only constant air currents are the fresh breezes along the sea coast.

A lake in the Pirin mountains, one of the country's beauty spots.

LAKES AND SPRINGS

Sources of water abound in Bulgaria, yet the country has limited water supplies. Except for the river Danube, not one of the 490 or more rivers is navigable.

The Bulgarian lakes are noted for their beauty. Those along the Black Sea coast attract tourists and nature lovers. The mud of these lakes is believed to have medicinal qualities and is processed by the pharmaceutical industry. Sreburna Lake by the Danube is the habitat of rare birds such as the pink pelican and the wild swan. The high mountainous lakes of glacial origin are also tourist attractions.

Many mineral springs—hot, warm, or cold—are found all over the country. Their perceived medicinal properties have also attracted the pharmaceutical industry.

FLORA AND FAUNA

Bulgaria is a paradise for botanists and nature lovers. It is home to over 12,000 plant species and 18,000 animal species. Some, such as the Rila cowslip and the Pirin poppy, are unique to Bulgaria, and the Bulgarian oil-bearing rose is the only descendant of the Persian rose surviving in Europe.

Plant and animal relics of bygone geological eras are also to be found. These include the Strandja periwinkle, the white and black spruce, and the sycamore. Deciduous oak, elm, and beech, together with coniferous pine, fir, and spruce, are the dominant varieties of trees. The woods are the habitat of wild animals: deer, boar, fox, wolf, mountain goat, bear, rabbit, and pheasant. There are 11 national parks and nearly 90 wildlife reserves in the country, with 330 protected plant species and 400 protected animal species.

Oil-bearing roses thrive in the fertile soils of southern Bulgaria.

TOWN AND COUNTRY

Bulgarians live mainly in industrialized cities or in villages with an agrarian economic base. This system of settlement has evolved from centuries of development, largely influenced by the variety of geographical conditions.

Bulgarian villages, found all over the country, are older and far more numerous than the cities. The biggest and most prosperous villages are concentrated in the fertile plains of northern and southern Bulgaria. There is not a big difference between the lifestyle of the villagers and that of the city dwellers. But the mountain villages tend to be smaller, poorer, and clustered closer to one another. Their populations have dwindled substantially, because young people have migrated to the cities in search of employment and cultural diversion.

It was during the 19th century that urbanization became especially marked. The process accelerated during the Socialist period, when the country developed an industrial base.

SOFIA Bulgaria's capital lies in an enclosed valley at the foot of Mount Vitosha and has a population of 1,167,000, which is 13% of Bulgaria's total population. It was built on the site of an ancient Roman fortress, the remains of which can still be seen in the underpasses in the city center. Architecturally, Sofia is a mix of turn-of-the century Baroque buildings, Byzantine-style churches, a sprinkling of mosques or Turkish baths, and massive concrete Socialist structures dating from the 1950s.

Sofia became the capital in 1879, after Bulgaria gained independence from the Turkish empire. At the time, the young capital was no bigger than a village. Today, however, it is the biggest city in the country, a major industrial center, a cultural center, and the seat of government.

PLOVDIV This city lies on both sides of the Maritsa river in the middle of the Thracian plain. It is Bulgaria's second largest and perhaps most beautiful city. Cobblestone streets twist up the hillsides in the Old Town. Plovdiv has an important industrial base and is known for its International Trade Fair.

VARNA This is Bulgaria's third largest city and its second biggest port. Known to the ancient Greeks as Odessus, Varna is now an industrial, transportation, medical, and cultural center of national importance. Several tourist resorts line the beaches adjacent to the city. In the summer domestic and international tourists flock to these resorts, as well as to the International Ballet Theater Tournament and the music and drama festivals.

A street scene in the capital city of Sofia.

HISTORY

THE MASS MIGRATIONS OF THE SLAVS to the Balkan peninsula during the sixth and seventh centuries spearheaded the founding of the Bulgarian state. Before that, ancient Thracian, Greek, Roman, and Byzantine civilizations had left their mark on the country's cultural heritage.

The name Bulgaria is not Slavic, but originated from the nomadic tribe of Bulgars that came from the steppes north of the Black Sea.

The Bulgars were warriors, disciplined and obedient to their chief, Khan Asparuh, who led them in seizing Slavic lands in Moesia and Little Scythia on the northeast fringe of Byzantium. The mighty Byzantine empire was compelled to recognize the authority of the Bulgars in the lands they had captured.

Opposite: **A corridor in Rila monastery, one of the oldest buildings in southern Bulgaria.**

Below: **Thracian ruins, uncovered by archeologists in the city of Plovdiv.**

FIRST FOR THE SLAVS

In the year A.D. 681, a treaty was signed in which the Byzantine rulers agreed to pay tribute to the newly founded state of Slavs and Bulgars, known as the First Bulgarian Kingdom. This was a precedent and an achievement for the seven Slavic tribes, made possible by the vigorous alliance with the Bulgars.

Because Bulgaria then controlled major roads linking Eastern Europe and Asia with the interior of the European continent, it became the focal point of strife and confrontation between East and West in medieval Europe. Bulgaria's first decades were marked by a life-and-death struggle for survival against the Byzantine empire, and

this gave the multiethnic tribes a sense of unity. The country became a barrier against nomadic incursions from the northeast. Bulgaria thus contributed greatly to political stability in this part of Europe.

Statues of Cyril and Methodius, in front of the National Library in Sofia. The two theologian brothers developed the first Slavic language and the Cyrillic alphabet, still used by all Slavs of the Eastern church.

CLASSICAL HERITAGE

The civic peace of the country was protected by a severe legal code introduced by Khan Krum, remembered in history as Krum the Terrible. According to his laws, defamation was punished by death; robbery by breaking the anklebones; and denying alms to a beggar by seizing property in the name of the ruler.

The amalgamation of the Slavs and Bulgars was finally accomplished with the adoption of Orthodox Christianity by Boris I in the ninth century. This memorable event came after long negotiations with the Church of Rome and the Church in Constantinople, enabling the Bulgarian Church to win a considerable degree of independence.

The link with Constantinople in terms of religion and politics gave the Bulgarians a classical heritage, a religious structure, Byzantine political and legal concepts, and the best defined national culture in Europe at that period.

The leaders of the Bulgarian state were well aware that the Christianization of the country could lead to a Byzantine cultural conquest of Bulgaria. This is why Prince Boris eagerly adopted the Slavic letters created by Cyril and Methodius and worked out a plan for spreading the liturgy and learning—not in Greek, but in the spoken Slavic language of his country.

Thus the Bulgarian national identity was forged—through the new state religion, the growth of education and its spread to widening circles, and through the development of a Bulgarian literary language.

The First Bulgarian Kingdom reached the zenith of its political, military, social, and cultural development during the reign of Tzar Simeon (889–927), known as "the Bulgarian Charlemagne." He made a determined effort to oust the Byzantine empire from the Balkan peninsula and gain recognition for himself as an emperor in the medieval family of Christian monarchs.

GOLDEN AGE OF CULTURE

This period was marked by a surge toward political and religious equality with Byzantium, territorial expansion of Bulgaria over the greater part of the Balkans, and by a flowering of Bulgarian culture.

The new capital city of Preslav was renowned for its magnificent architecture. Along with Okhrida at the opposite end of Tzar Simeon's empire, Preslav emerged as a leading center of Slavic literature and culture.

Clement of Okhrida and his students encouraged an enlightened approach to cultural development. Writers of the period were intensely conscious of their role as champions of the new Slavic culture. Having gained much from Byzantine culture, Bulgaria in turn influenced the Serbs, Russians, and Romanians.

Crown Prince Boris (1894–1943) came to the throne as Boris III. His son succeeded him as Simeon II, but the Bulgarian monarchy was abolished in 1946.

The distinctive stone walls of Veliko Turnovo, which reached its glory in the 13th century as the capital and fortress of the Second Bulgarian Kingdom.

SURVIVAL AND TRIUMPH

After Tzar Simeon's death, the Bulgarian kingdom plunged into a deep social and political crisis and eventually fell to Byzantium. The eastern Bulgarian provinces and the capital Preslav were taken in A.D. 971. The southeastern provinces, with Okhrida as the new state capital, were for a long time successful in staving off defeat, but in 1018 they were finally conquered by the Byzantine emperor Basil II, who took the title of the Bulgar Slayer.

For over a century and a half of Byzantine colonization, the Bulgarian people suffered excessive taxation, systematic destruction of their literature and their cultural monuments, and other forms of abuse. Yet throughout those years, they kept alive a spirit of freedom and resistance. One after another, uprisings and rebellions against the Byzantine rulers shook the foundations of the empire. The armed resistance of the Bulgarian feudal lords was backed by the mass Bogomil movement—a religious and social organization whose ideology embodied strongly felt anti-Byzantine trends.

In 1185 the Boyar brothers Ivan and Petar Asen led a movement to free Bulgarians in the lands between the Danube and the Balkan mountains. This led to the establishment of the Second Bulgarian Kingdom, with the Balkan fortress of Veliko Turnovo as the capital. Kaloyan, who succeeded the Asen brothers, completed the liberation of the Bulgarian population of Thrace, the Rhodope region, and Macedonia. His diplomacy led to the recognition of the kingdom by Byzantium and papal Rome.

The restored kingdom's hour of triumph came during the reign of Ivan Asen II (1218–1241). His skillful diplomatic maneuvers expanded Bulgaria's territory. Once again it stretched "from shore to shore," from the Black Sea to the Adriatic, as it had during Tzar Simeon's Golden Age.

Another view of Veliko Turnovo. In its heyday, it was a city of economic and cultural supremacy.

A SECOND ROME

Veliko Turnovo was extolled as the city "saved by God" and called "a second Rome" and "a new Constantinople." The vast Bulgarian state saw a new cultural and economic upsurge. It extended its political and trade relations with a number of European states. There was a massive construction of churches, fortresses, and bridges. Aristocratic patronage of trades and the arts flourished as never before.

Yet by the second half of the 13th century, Bulgaria faced another grave political crisis. A peasant revolt and attacks from Mongol tribes had weakened it, making it easy prey for the new great power that arose in the east of Europe—the Ottoman empire.

These buildings with balconies are fine examples of National Revival architecture of the 19th century.

STRUGGLE FOR THE NATION

In the last decade of the 14th century, the Ottoman empire conquered the Bulgarian people and their divided rulers. The independent development of the Bulgarian state was interrupted for nearly five centuries. Hundreds of settlements, fortresses, churches, and monasteries were reduced to ashes by the Turkish invaders. The political and spiritual elite of the Bulgarian people were exiled or exterminated, and the clergy was dispersed or ruthlessly repressed. The national Bulgarian church was subordinated to Constantinople. Bulgarians were excluded from local administration, and all of the country's resources were put at the disposal of the Ottoman war machine.

The conquest was marked by a wholesale slaughter of soldiers and civilians. Tens of thousands of Bulgarians were sold in the slave markets; thousands more sought refuge abroad; Christians were forced en masse to convert to Islam, or were compelled to move to the Asian parts of the Ottoman empire, to be replaced by Muslim Turks.

To some extent, this fanatic persecution of the Bulgarian "infidels" roused the national and religious feelings of the Bulgarian people, compelling them to define their national identity and to preserve their cultural traditions and values. This they succeeded in doing, against great odds. From the peasants in secluded mountain villages to the monks in the few surviving monasteries, all made their contributions. So too did the *haidouks* ("hai-DOOKS"), members of the spontaneous underground movement against Turkish domination.

By the 18th century, the spirit of the people was truly stirred—by the economic upsurge of the Bulgarian community within the Ottoman empire, by its commercial contacts with people from near and distant lands, and by the influence of the European Enlightenment.

Elegant cloisters of a town museum.

The first to spur the people on was Father Paisii from the Chilendar monastery on Mount Athos in Greece. In 1762 the monk completed his *Slav-Bulgarian History*, an ardent appeal to the Bulgarian people to cherish their language and culture, to take pride in their glorious historical past, and to fight for their liberation.

NATIONAL REVIVAL MOVEMENT

In the first half of the 19th century, the momentum for a national revival gathered pace. Schools and library clubs began to open up in the towns and villages. This gave an impetus to literature and journalism. Church and urban architecture also flourished, along with the visual arts.

In 1870 the Ottoman government finally gave in to the long and determined struggle of the Bulgarians for a national church, separate from the Greek Patriarchate.

The independent Church of the Bulgarian Exarchate became the first national political institution, one that was recognized by Turkey.

LEVSKI: APOSTLE OF FREEDOM

The purest figure of the liberation movement was Vassil Levski (1837–1873), called the apostle of freedom by peasants and scholars alike. Levski was a saint of the revolution. Guided by an unflinching confidence in the Bulgarian national spirit, he decided his country could only be liberated with the participation of the entire population. He therefore devoted his boundless energy and organizational talent to underground work in towns and villages throughout Bulgaria.

Apart from setting up the local revolutionary committees, Levski drew up the statutes of the organization. This was a political program of true democracy. Here is how he envisaged the democratic future of the country:

"In our Bulgaria things will be different from how they are in Turkey now. All the nationalities in our country, Turks, Jews, and others, will live under the same pure and sacred laws."

"There will be no king in Bulgaria, but 'popular rule' and to each 'his due' ... A free and pure republic."

"We yearn to see our fatherland free, and when that day comes I will be content just to keep watch over the ducks at pasture."

Betrayed by a fellow Bulgarian and captured by the Turks, Levski was hanged outside Sofia on February 19, 1873. To this day, Bulgarians commemorate his death by laying flowers on the modest monument that marks the place of his execution.

Fantastic feats and acts of courage were performed by Bulgarians during the Liberation War of 1877–1878. They joined the Russian army and halted the Turkish onslaught by using as barricades tree trunks, rocks, and even the bodies of their dead comrades.

SLAUGHTER OF THE APRIL UPRISING

Nationalistic fervor led to an armed revolutionary campaign, known as the National Revival movement. It aimed at liberating Bulgaria from Ottoman domination and culminated in the April Uprising of 1876, which was suppressed with unprecedented cruelty and revenge. The Turkish army and irregular bands slaughtered men, women, and children. Some 80 villages and their inhabitants were reduced to ashes.

On their way to the gallows, the organizers of the revolt rejoiced that their goal had been achieved and expressed their faith in Slavic solidarity. One of them, the military commander Georgi Benkovski, exclaimed, "Such a mortal wound have I inflicted to the heart of the tyrant that he will never recover from it. As for Russia—she is now welcome!"

In 1877 Russia did declare war on the Ottoman empire, and thousands of Bulgarians volunteered their services. Finally, on March 3, 1878, Turkey signed a treaty of capitulation, recognizing Bulgaria's independence.

STRIFE FOR UNIFICATION

The San Stefano settlement ensured the political liberation of the Bulgarians in Moesia (between the Danube and the Balkan mountains), Northern Thrace, and Macedonia. Under its own church and state, the Bulgarian nation felt free, united, and on the threshold of a great future.

But the dream was shattered only five months later by the Berlin Congress of the European superpowers. To satisfy the claims of England and Austria, the Bulgarian state had three of its main provinces taken away, with only Moesia and the region around Sofia retaining their status.

ISSUE OVER MACEDONIA

Thrace, under the name of Eastern Rumelia, was returned to the Ottoman empire. Macedonia and the Aegean coast were also returned to the Ottoman empire, without any undertaking to protect the Bulgarian population. The decisions of the Berlin Congress thwarted aspirations for national unity and hindered for a long time Bulgaria's political, economic, and cultural development. It also planted the explosive "Macedonian Question" in European politics.

Bulgaria did not resign itself to the slicing up of the nation. The Eastern Rumelia province proclaimed its alliance with the principality of Bulgaria in 1885, and the population of Southern Thrace and Macedonia struggled determinedly for their liberty, but to no avail.

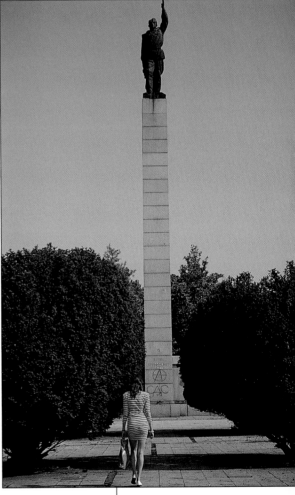

A young woman walks up to the War Memorial in the city of Burgas.

THE EXPLOSIVE MACEDONIAN QUESTION

The ethnic identity of the Macedonians has long been a controversial issue. Until the 19th century, "Macedonia" usually indicated a geographical area populated mainly by Bulgarians, with a mix of Greeks, Turks, Albanians, Gypsies, Armenians, Jews, and marginally, Serbs.

Many prominent figures of the National Revival were born in Macedonia, but always referred to themselves as Bulgarian. When the Berlin Congress of 1878 restored Macedonia to the Ottoman empire, its population loudly protested the separation from their "conationals." After the Balkan wars in the first two decades of this century, Macedonia was divided among Greece, Serbia, and Bulgaria. Forced population transfers followed, largely removing Slavic speakers from Greek Macedonia and Greek speakers from the rest of the territory. Today, over a quarter of the Bulgarian nation can trace its roots to Macedonia.

The notion of a distinct Macedonian nationality, with its own language and history, was introduced in this century by Tito's regime in the former Yugoslavia, with Stalin's approval. When the Yugoslav Federation broke up, the independent state of Macedonia was created in 1991. Bulgaria was the first country to give full recognition to the new state of Macedonia, despite vehement Greek protests. All the same, the Bulgarian people have been reluctant to acknowledge the existence of a Macedonian nationality, or to recognize the Macedonian language.

Bulgaria became a Communist state after 1944 and began to echo the Soviet Union in many spheres. But in some areas, such as central control of the arts, it has proved less restrictive than the former Soviet Union.

THE BALKAN WARS

Until World War II, Bulgaria pursued the dream of restoring the lands of the San Stefano Treaty, engaging in a series of ill-fated Balkan wars. After repelling a Serbian invasion only weeks after the unification of 1885, the young Bulgarian state formed a new alliance with Greece, Serbia, and Montenegro.

In the First Balkan War (1912), the allies forced Turkey to give up its remaining Balkan territories, but extremist nationalistic fervor split up the new alliance. This consequently led to the Second Balkan War (1913), fought by Bulgaria, Romania, Serbia, Greece, and Turkey. It ended in a national catastrophe for Bulgaria, as territory was lost.

World War I tore even more lands from the country and ruined its industry and agriculture, all of which resulted in a severe political crisis. Defeated and humiliated, Bulgaria completely lost faith in her nationalistic ideals.

IN THE SOVIET BLOC

During World War II, Bulgaria was a reluctant ally of Germany. It declared a symbolic war on Great Britain and the United States, but its government did not send troops into combat and declined to deport the Bulgarian Jews to the death camps of Poland.

In September 1944, while the Bulgarian government was conducting peace talks with the Allies, the Soviet Union declared war on Bulgaria. In conjunction with the Soviet offensive, power in Sofia was seized by a Communist-led coalition, called the Fatherland Front.

The stage was thus set for the communization of the country—a process that was completed two years later—despite resistance from democratic forces. Bulgaria then became known as the Soviet Union's most faithful ally, copying the twists and turns of Soviet policies. With the Communist Party in charge, pervasive state ownership became the order of the day and all aspects of the economy came under state control.

Nevertheless, the Bulgarian model has in some ways been significantly different from the Soviet system. It has paid more careful attention to agriculture, raising the rural population's living standards, and the country's achievements in foreign trade have been fairly impressive.

This monument to Lenin in Sofia was pulled down during Bulgaria's "gentle revolution."

THORNY PATH TO DEMOCRACY

Bulgaria's "gentle revolution" began with the removal from office of the dictator Todor Zhivkov in November 1989. Zhivkov's fall set off a wave of rallies. Tens of thousands of demonstrators converged on the central squares of the capital and the big cities—to demand free elections and the end of the regime.

A peaceful group at one of the major demonstrations held in the country after 1989.

HOW NEW GROUPS AVOIDED SCRUTINY

In 1988 something new developed in the modern political life of the nation. Various "informal organizations" started springing up, spearheading the drive for democratic change.

These "informal groups" were so called in order to avoid harassment or scrutiny by the authorities. They included an ecological association in Sofia and Ruse called Ecoglasnost, a club at the University of Sofia that supported glasnost and democracy, writers' groups in Plovdiv and Sofia, an independent confederation of labor that followed the pattern of Poland's Solidarity party, a committee for religious rights and freedom of conscience and spiritual values in Veliko Turnovo, and others. They proved to be too widespread for the Communist regime to eliminate.

After the fall of the dictator Todor Zhivkov, the existing informal organizations and the fast-growing opposition political parties formed the Union of Democratic Forces. The UDF committed itself to the peaceful dismantling of the totalitarian system and a transition to democracy and market economy.

Two campaigners who became known to the general public were Zhelyu Zhelev and Petur Beron, the chairman and vice-chairman of the UDF. Beron was a founding member of Ecoglasnost.

The summer of 1990 was an uneasy time for politicians in power, as the people, the students, and the country's intellectuals came out in their thousands to seek a better mandate for their country.

To the credit of those involved—the reforming wing of the Communist Party, which took over from Zhivkov's old guard, and the young alliance of democratic organizations—Bulgaria managed to break away from Communist rule without bloodshed and violence.

Lengthy negotiations went on between the reforming Communist Party, renamed the Bulgarian Socialist Party (BSP), and the Union of Democratic Forces (UDF). The talks led to an agreement on how elections for a Grand National Assembly were to be held. The assembly's task was to work out a new democratic constitution, and this was accomplished in 1991.

After the initial political elation over the first taste of freedom, the country was confronted with a far more daunting prospect. The wounds of a nation divided over its Communist past had to be healed, the economy was in bad shape and needed reviving, and the country had to be made a hospitable part of the new unified Europe.

GOVERNMENT

BULGARIA IS A PARLIAMENTARY REPUBLIC with an emerging democracy. For nearly half a decade, the constitution guaranteed the Communist Party the exclusive right to total political power. Today, power has been handed to the people, who exert it directly or through freely elected legislative and executive bodies.

WINDS OF CHANGE

The democratic process began in 1989 when a group of younger members of the Bulgarian Communist Party failed to see eye to eye with the "old guard." The young blood was influenced by political changes in the Soviet Union under President Gorbachev. They pressed for a more open domestic policy. The dictator, Todor Zhivkov, was forced to resign and was replaced by Petar Mladenov, his foreign minister, who had been leading the drive for reform.

The party changed its name to the Bulgarian Socialist Party (BSP) and commented publicly on the corruption and failings of the old regime. Although the BSP refused to part with property accumulated by the regime, it was evident that it was no longer a solid dictatorial power. Splinter groups formed, pressing for reform and public accountability. Some of these groups became independent political parties.

The young opposition began to gather huge support. In the streets, especially in Sofia and other big cities, vast numbers attended their rallies, demanding that the Communists step down from power.

Above: **A political celebration in Plovdiv.**

Opposite: **Massive rallies such as this heralded free elections in 1990.**

HISTORY OF THE COMMUNIST PARTY

For 45 years, the Bulgarian Communist Party had a constitutionally guaranteed right to power in the country. It commanded all aspects of social, economic, cultural, and educational life. Membership in the party was high compared to other ruling Communist parties. As a political power, it has a long and tumultuous history.

Founded as a workers' social-democratic party in 1891, it was renamed the Bulgarian Communist Party (BCP) in 1919. Its Communist symbols were even incorporated into the state coat of arms (see below). It became a cofounder and an active member of the Third Communist International. After the seizure of power by the military-royalist coalition in 1923, the leadership of the BCP fled to Moscow. Until World War II, the party led a double life as an underground political force within the country, while its surviving leaders were sheltered abroad.

During World War II, the underground BCP committed acts of sabotage and assassinated police officials and fascist functionaries, but did not organize a general insurrection. The BCP's road to power began with two concurrent events: Soviet troops crossed into Bulgaria in September 1944 and Sofia was seized by the leftist political alliance of the Fatherland Front.

Once in power, the BCP mobilized the army and the economy for the battle against Germany, purged the Fatherland Front coalition of its competitors, and earned Soviet respect as an effective and loyal ally. From this point on, until the emergence of democracy in 1989, the history of the BCP closely followed that of Soviet political life, and its political grip remained firm and virtually uncontested.

The period before the first free elections of 1990 was a momentous occasion for the people. Yet after the elections, there was a feeling of letdown, as the Bulgarian Socialist Party managed to come back into power. All the same, a wide spectrum of political representation was introduced into the Bulgarian Parliament.

FREE ELECTIONS 45 YEARS LATER

For Bulgarians over the voting age of 18, the 1990 parliamentary elections were a most exciting political experience. Yet the elections were also the cause of profound disappointment. Despite massive public demonstrations of unity by the opposition coalition, the anticommunist votes got dispersed among parties that did not muster the necessary 3% of the public vote. The majority of the seats in the Grand National Assembly were won by the Bulgarian Socialist Party, but Bulgarians did not resign themselves to continued rule by the BSP.

Shortly after the elections, students at the University of Sofia went on strike, something without precedent in the history of the nation. The students demanded an investigation into the fairness of the elections, and the resignation of the Socialist president Petar Mladenov, who had called out army tanks in answer to widespread demonstrations. The strike spread throughout the country, and before long Mladenov resigned. Parliament was in deadlock over the election of a new president since no party could muster the necessary majority.

In the political summer of 1990, a unique movement developed with the aim of forestalling a Socialist victory. Led by students and a number of the country's intellectuals, Bulgarians pitched tents in the center of the capital, forming what came to be known as the "City of Truth." Over the next several months, the demonstration grew in size and power, numbering at its height 6,000 to 7,000 people.

NEW CONSTITUTION

In the summer of 1990 the newly elected Grand National Assembly (Parliament) started its work on a new democratic constitution. Charged with a historical mission, this Bulgarian parliament had twice as many representatives as the regular assembly.

The 480 representatives of the Bulgarian people faced a daunting task. They had to work out the most important and lasting piece of legislation for a nation that was bitterly divided in its political allegiances. They had to relearn the principles of dialogue and negotiation. They had to provide the legal basis for a thorough economic reform, which no other former Communist country had accomplished to date, and they had to do it fast, since the country was in danger of falling into a state of anarchy and economic chaos.

Bulgaria's parliament building, the National Assembly, in Sofia.

The head of state, President Zhelyu Zhelev, has been a leader in the Union of Democratic Forces since its early days.

POWERS OF THE PRESIDENT

After Petar Mladenov resigned as head of state, there was a deadlock over the presidency. The functions of the president had to be spelled out. They are more limited than those of the president of the United States.

The Bulgarian president is the commander in chief of the army and has the power to veto parliamentary decisions. He approves the Cabinet but does not appoint it. He or she is elected by a direct and secret ballot for a five-year term.

Candidates for this post are backed by their political parties before elections, but once in office, the president tries to set aside narrow party allegiances, and act as a unifying force. This is because he is largely a symbolic figure, representing national unity.

PRECARIOUS BALANCE

The president of the Republic of Bulgaria is Zhelyu Zhelev, professor of philosophy at the University of Sofia. In the last presidential elections in 1992, Bulgarians also voted for their first woman vice-president, Blaga Dimitrova, a writer and poet, and a charismatic figure in the Union of Democratic Forces. She has since resigned.

Bulgaria's legislation is worked out in the National Assembly, the parliamentary body of the country, which has one chamber. Its members are reelected by the direct secret vote of all Bulgarians over 18 years old.

The National Assembly has 240 representatives, with the Bulgarian Socialist Party currently holding an absolute majority, followed by the Union of Democratic Forces. Since the first free elections, the balance of power has been very precarious. Coalitions are short-lived, and members of parliament often switch allegiances.

THE CABINET

The supreme executive body for home and foreign affairs is the Council of Ministers (the Cabinet). It is voted in by the National Assembly. In the current trying period of economic transition and cultural and moral crisis, few cabinets have lasted long. Bulgaria is divided into nine administrative regions, each of them subdivided into smaller municipalities that are self-governing legal entities.

Parliament controls national broadcasting by its power to appoint and dismiss the heads of radio and television.

ECONOMY

THE COLLAPSE OF THE BERLIN WALL in 1989 ushered in change throughout the whole of Eastern Europe. In Bulgaria, the Socialist economy collapsed, and the country is now on a bumpy road of trying to reform a centralized type of production into a market economy.

The Socialist system had left the country with an unwieldy economic structure and a daunting national debt. It had concentrated too much on heavy industry when it lacked energy supplies and natural resources. By the end of the 1980s, industrial and agricultural production fell steeply. Inflation and unemployment rates soared.

SHOCK THERAPY REFORM

The new governments have been trying to mitigate the crisis by a program of economic reforms, started in 1991, and based on monetary "shock therapy." According to this model, inflation is curbed by a drastic increase in all prices and interest rates, and by withdrawing state subsidies from ineffective enterprises.

While these measures did eventually succeed in stabilizing the annual inflation rate, they badly affected both the economic development of the country and the living standards of the people. For the period 1985–1992, there was a 40% fall in production. Over 70% of Bulgaria's population now live at or below the poverty line.

Revitalizing production in the new private sector was felt to be the best hope for the economy. Small to medium-size state enterprises were the first to be privatized. The government returned some private property that it seized in the 1940s. It has also made an effort to attract foreign investment.

Above: **The harbor in the city of Varna.**

Opposite: **A worker in a field of tobacco plants. Tobacco is one of the country's major exports.**

A factory in central Bulgaria. Heavy industry, once developed to the neglect of light industry, is now virtually immobilized.

INDUSTRY BY THE BOOK

Before World War II, industrial enterprises were mostly those of textile production, food processing, and woodworking. There was no heavy industry to speak of, as power sources and technical facilities were rudimentary. After the war, under Soviet influence, the economy was reorganized after the Soviet model and tied to it.

Bulgaria wanted to catch up with the industrialized nations, and to see a better balance in economic structure, a more even development of the country's different regions, and the setting up of heavy industry. Consequently, there was a concentration on heavy machine-building and on chemical and metallurgy plants, even though the country lacked both natural resources and export markets.

At the same time, the government curtailed the development of light industries, despite the fact that in this area the country had considerable experience and a good international reputation.

ECOLOGICAL PRICE OF INDUSTRIALIZATION

When Bulgaria's heavy industries were being enthusiastically set up, nobody considered the threat they might pose to the environment. Today, in cities with a concentration of heavy industry, in particular metallurgy, chemicals, and cement, the threat has become a disastrous reality.

The air in these cities is polluted from industrial emission; the rivers are full of raw sewage, heavy metals, and detergents; the forests are damaged from air pollution and acid rain; and once-fertile soils are contaminated with heavy metals from nearby metallurgical plants.

The ecological balance is badly disturbed in over half the country. About 40% of Bulgaria's population live in areas with a dangerous level of pollution. The situation is grave in Ruse, Devnya, Dimitrovgrad, Burgas, and in the Sofia suburb of Kremikovtzi. Residents of these areas have shown a serious rise in respiratory and other pollution-related diseases, with children being the worst-affected.

The price it had to pay was high. Bulgaria could not afford to keep up with the latest technological developments of heavy industry. Nor could it compete in the international market on price and quality. Its huge plants soon became outdated. To upgrade them, the government had to resort to high-interest loans, which added to the fast-growing national debt.

Mothers of small children turn up in force at an anti-pollution rally in Sofia, protesting against the dangers of high levels of industrial waste.

On top of all this, most heavy industry was concentrated in the big regional centers of Sofia, Plovdiv, Varna, Ruse, Burgas, and Vidin. This meant that cities suffered from overpopulation and acute housing problems, while the once-thriving villages and small towns in the southeast and northwest declined.

Today Bulgaria's economy still depends on industry. But except for the manufacture of pharmaceutical products and electronic and optical appliances, heavy industry is practically immobilized. Light industry, on the other hand, is recovering fast. Bulgaria's textiles and knitwear have a good reputation both in the domestic and international markets. The production of foodstuffs, wine, and tobacco is also gaining ground.

An orchard in southern Bulgaria. Only a small proportion of the country's arable land is being cultivated.

MISTAKES IN AGRICULTURE

Agriculture accounts for only a small part of the national product. Yet Bulgaria has fertile land and a mild climate well able to support the growing of grain, oilseeds, vegetables, fruit, and tobacco. Over a third of the arable land is devoted to grain production. Bulgaria is the world's fourth largest tobacco exporter. The abundant mountain pastures are perfect for the raising of livestock. Despite all this, agriculture is in a deeper crisis than the industrial sector of the economy.

It all started in 1946 when a Soviet model of agriculture was implemented. The estates of large landowners were seized and nationalized, and smaller landowners and stockbreeders were forced into agricultural cooperatives. Consequently, property was destroyed and animals slaughtered. Effectively deprived of their property, many small farmers and agricultural workers began to move to the cities in search of independence and better fortunes.

LAW OF THE LAND As a result of these drastic measures, Bulgaria's fragmented agriculture was modernized and became large-scale. But the problems soon grew. For one thing, there followed an acute shortage of manpower.

The country today can no longer meet the needs of its textile and food-processing industries. Bulgaria, traditionally a surplus food producer, started having to import basic foods.

To resolve the crisis and return the land to its previous owners, the Bulgarian Parliament voted in a new Law of the Land in 1992. This law created a free market, with the aim of allowing landowners to buy and sell land, and to form associations and corporations.

AGRICULTURE IN LIMBO The Socialist farm cooperatives, now seen as parasitic state concerns, were dismantled. Yet three years later, few Bulgarians have been given back their land and even fewer have found the means to cultivate what land has been returned.

Forty years of civil construction and intensive industrialization have significantly changed the map of the country, and it is not easy trying to restore to owners the precise plot of land they once owned. Migration has further slowed the transfer. As a result, only a small part of Bulgaria's arable land is used to its full potential.

Tobacco leaves left to dry. Oriental tobacco is a major export.

The yellow trams of Sofia are a familiar sight on the city streets.

TRANSPORTATION

While the overall economy of the country may be in shambles, Bulgaria has a modern transportation system. Because international commercial routes cross the Balkan peninsula, connecting Europe to Asia and Africa, comprehensive rail and road systems have developed in Bulgaria.

In addition, there are several international airports, as well as maritime transportation along the Danube and across the Black Sea.

TRAVEL BY TRAIN Most of the country's railroad system was built just before World War II. By 1992, the railways totalled 4,076 miles (6,558 km), with more than 50% of the system now electrified. The big cities are connected by express trains. Most Bulgarians still prefer to travel by train, since it is cheap and reliable. Several international express trains also pass through the country.

BY ROAD AND BY WATER Bulgaria's road system is not too well maintained, as the cost of road construction is high. Plans for completing a national expressway have been set aside, with only 172 miles (277 km) of the expressway completed. The country has 22,943 miles (36,915 km) of roads.

Bulgaria has two main waterways: the Black Sea, connecting the country with the Mediterranean Sea and the rest of the world, and the Danube, the gateway to Central Europe. Bulgaria's merchant fleet is fairly large. It includes railcar carriers, chemical carriers, container ships, oil tankers, and ships carrying refrigerated and bulk cargo. There are also smaller passenger vessels for tourist use.

AIRPORTS AND AIRLINES Bulgaria has three international airports—in Sofia, Varna, and Burgas. The airport in Sofia is also the oldest civil airport, with the busiest air traffic. There are future plans for building a new modern airport in Sofia. The main airline is Balkan Air.

A lone car on one of Bulgaria's better roads.

BULGARIANS

ETHNIC BULGARIANS MAKE UP 85% of the population, and they are traditionally Eastern Orthodox Christians. The most sizable minority group are the Turks, accounting for 9.7%. Next come the Gypsies, at 3.4% of the population. The remaining 2% are Pomaks, Armenians, Jews, Russians, Tartars, Romanians, Greeks, and Karakachans, who are Hellenized Thracians.

This population breakdown may not appear too diverse ethnically, but the lands of Bulgaria have been, in the words of the writer Konstantin Paustovski, "the route of nations," and "a place of continuous bivouacs." The "maternal stock" of today's Bulgarians therefore goes back to the ancient Thracians, Illyrians, Bulgars, and Slavs. The Byzantine and Ottoman conquerors of the Bulgarian lands have also left their mark on the ethnic and cultural makeup of the nation.

Left: **A monk in a monastery yard. Most Bulgarians are Eastern Orthodox Christians.**

Opposite: **A potter at work, showing the blend of soberness and taciturnity that appears to characterize the Bulgarians.**

A Gypsy with a performing bear. Gypsies are the second largest minority in Bulgaria, but they are among the poorest in the country.

MAKING OF THE BULGARIAN PEOPLE

Thracians were the oldest inhabitants of the Bulgarian lands, going as far back as the second millennium before Christ. Then came the Romans. Both civilizations have left their mark. To this day there are Roman roads, baths, and amphitheaters in the country.

The Slavs came to the Balkan peninsula in the sixth and seventh centuries. They were good farmers and stockbreeders. This large ethnic group then assimilated with the Bulgars and the Thracians. The Bulgars, who had arrived in the late seventh century, were nomads from the steppes by the Volga river. Of Turanian origin, they allied themselves with the Slavs against the Byzantine empire, laying the beginnings of the Bulgarian state and nation.

A DISTINCT CULTURE

In the long periods of Byzantine and Ottoman rule, the Bulgarian people resisted attempts at assimilation. They succeeded in preserving their language, culture, belief system, and lifestyle. The Bulgarian culture of today bears some Turkish and Greek traces, but has largely kept its distinct character.

Bulgarians have shown themselves to be fairly tolerant in ethnic and religious matters, which is commendable, especially in a European region with a turbulent history that has been traversed by many tribes and peoples. Bulgaria is one of the few countries from the former Eastern Bloc where the collapse of Communism did not trigger off ethnic bloodshed. The only shadow is the uneasy divide between the ethnic Bulgarians and the Turkish minority.

THE PROVERBIAL BULGARIAN CHARACTER

ALTRUISM: Do a good deed and cast it into the sea.

DETERMINATION: The dogs are barking, but the caravan marches on.

FATALISM: If evil does not come, worse may arrive.

FEMALE: A woman is an iron shirt.

FRIENDS: For a lean year, a relative; for a misfortune, a friend.

INFALLIBILITY: God is not sinless—He created the world.

NECESSITY : When there's no work to be found, join the army.

RESERVE: As with the tzar, so with fire—neither go too close nor too far.

RESPONSIBILITY: Where there are many shepherds, many sheep are lost.

SELF-IMPORTANCE: An empty bag weighs more than a full one.

SELF-INTEREST: The dog barks to guard itself—not the village.

WEAKNESS: The Greek will fail because he boasts, the Bulgarian because he is pig-headed.

WORK: Work left for later is finished by the Devil.

The rugged individualism of the Bulgarians is reflected in their sayings and proverbs, refined over the centuries.

Bulgarian Muslims converse in a mosque that was recently restored.

THE BULGARIAN TURKS

The Turks are descendants of the Ottomans. They are Sunni Muslim by belief and speak the Turkish language. Most of them live in tightknit communities in the northeastern and southcentral parts of the country.

The traditional occupation of the Bulgarian Turks is agriculture, especially the cultivation of the well-known Oriental tobacco. The lifestyle of those in the rural areas is highly traditional.

There has been mutual suspicion between the Turks and the ethnic Bulgarians ever since the days of Ottoman rule.

AREA OF TENSION Relations became particularly strained in the 1980s. Bulgarian political commentators went so far as to argue that eventual Turkish separatism would give Turkey an excuse to intervene and turn Bulgaria into another Cyprus. Others pointed to the high birth rates of the Turks, raising the fear that the Bulgarians would become a minority in their own country.

During the nationalistic campaign of the Zhivkov government, the Turks were given the difficult alternative of surrendering their cultural identity or leaving the land they had inhabited for centuries.

But in recent years, both sides have shown a high degree of diplomacy in dealing with these tensions. Today the ethnic Turkish party, the Movement for Rights and Freedoms, is a recognized parliamentary power with a decisive voice in the legislative and political life of the country.

WHY THE POMAKS CHANGED THEIR FAITH

The Pomaks are a small group of Bulgarian-speaking Muslims who live in the Rhodope mountains. They are descendants of Bulgarians who had changed their faith from Christianity to Islam, either voluntarily or by force, during Ottoman rule. There is a rather unusual reason behind this. The Rhodope mountains used to be a favorite hunting ground for the Turkish sultan, and the Pomaks were often called upon to serve the royal hunting parties. But Muslim tradition stipulated that only believers in Islam could serve the sultan, so there followed a sustained effort to change the faith of these mountain people.

In one of its cultural campaigns of the early 1970s, the Communist government also forced the Pomaks to change their Turkish-Arabic names to Slavic "equivalents." The term "Pomak" was banned. Fortunately, no government decision could erase the cultural traditions of these people. Most Pomaks today still live in isolated mountain villages and have preserved their folk songs, customs, and their old handicrafts of wool-weaving and rug-making.

LEFT OUT IN THE COLD

A Pomak concentrates on his woodwork.

Accounting for 3.4% of the population, the Gypsies are the second largest minority in Bulgaria, yet they have little stake in the country. They speak their own language, Roma, but this has absorbed many Bulgarian words.

Gypsies used to live in caravans, which roamed the countryside. A small number of them still travel in the old-style caravans, and a few keep performing bears, hoping to collect a few coins during their stops in towns. Today most Gypsies live under poor or slum conditions on the outskirts of the big cities. They are undereducated and have high unemployment rates. Their life expectancy is much shorter than the average Bulgarian's.

A succession of Bulgarian governments have failed to deal with the plight of the Gypsies. A group called Roma was recently formed with the aims of raising the consciousness of this ethnic group and finding political ways of improving their lot.

49

THE OTHER MINORITIES

Apart from the Gypsies and the Pomaks, two other minority groups stand out. The Armenians came to Bulgaria in the early 20th century, driven away from their native land in the Caucasus Mountains after mass slaughters by the Turks. They are city-dwellers, speaking their own unique language and with their own Armenian Gregorian Church. Traditionally the Armenians do exquisite craftwork.

Mother and children in a Gypsy slum area in Plovdiv.

The Bulgarian Greeks live mostly in the cities along the Black Sea coast and in the bigger cities in south Bulgaria. They are descendants of old Greek colonists. Although some speak Greek within the family, their culture and lifestyle differ little from the Bulgarians'.

HOW THE BULGARIAN JEWS WERE SAVED

Few people are aware that the Bulgarian people saved 48,000 Jews during World War II. Bulgaria was then an ally of Nazi Germany and received territorial favors at the expense of Romania, Yugoslavia, and Greece.

Under German pressure, the government of the day introduced some halfhearted anti-Semitic measures. The population, however, responded with sympathy and support for the Jews.

When the Jews of Sofia were expelled to the countryside, the population of the capital tried to stop them from reaching the railway station and subsequently demonstrated in front of the King's palace.

In 1943 the Nazis finally reached an agreement with the Bulgarian Commissar for Jewish Affairs to deport 6,000 "leading Jews" to the Treblinka death camp in Poland. But none of these Jews ever left the country. Leading intellectuals raised an outcry in the media against the plan. Church officials and ordinary farmers from north Bulgaria threatened to lie down on the railway tracks to stop the deportation trains.

The chief rabbi of Sofia was hidden by Stephan of Sofia, a senior church official, who declared publicly that "God had determined the Jewish fate, and men had no right to torture Jews, and to persecute them."

Faced with such determined and widespread opposition, the government revoked the order, and Jews already taken into custody were released. The day of March 10, when the death trains were supposed to roll out, came to be known in Bulgaria as the "miracle of the Jewish people."

The Armenians are by tradition goldsmiths, watchmakers, shoemakers, and the like.

FEWER CHILDREN BORN

Since the beginning of the century, Bulgarians have been discouraged from having too many children. This was due to the practice of small peasant landholding, along with the custom of inheritance, in which all offspring were given a share of the land.

A low birth rate was the trend by the time of World War II. Bulgarian women having to work contributed to this trend. Even government programs of the 1960s and 1980s, which offered family allowances and maternity leave arrangements, failed to raise the birth rate. Today, with soaring unemployment, families are more hesitant than ever to have children.

In 1991 the population of Bulgaria reached nearly nine million. The following year, this figure was half a million lower, because of the low birth rate and intensive emigration.

The size, age, and ethnic makeup of Bulgaria's population have been affected by its migration patterns since the beginning of the century. During the Balkan wars, ethnic cleansing in neighboring Turkey, Greece, and Serbia sent huge waves of Bulgarian refugees into Bulgaria.

On the other hand, some Bulgarian Greeks left to settle in Greece between 1924 and 1926. In the 1940s Bulgarian Jews and Armenians left for Israel and the Armenian Republic. Under an agreement with the Turkish government, some 130,000 Bulgarian Turks migrated to Turkey between 1968 and 1978.

Bulgaria's population figures fell further in the years that followed, the result of two big emigration waves. The first of these was the "big trip" of the Bulgarian Turks from 1985 to 1989, the result of an infamous campaign by the last Communist government over the Turkish question. The Turks were forced to change their names to Slavic ones, prohibited from speaking Turkish in public, and banned from circumcising their male children, which is a ritual required by Islam.

Those who protested were forced to leave the country. The size of the exodus exceeded all expectations, numbering more than 300,000.

These Bulgarian Turks, arriving in Turkey as refugees, are grateful to have landed on Turkish soil. Faced with harsh measures back home, they were among 300,000 who chose to leave Bulgaria.

BRAIN DRAIN TO THE WEST

Throughout the 1990s, there has been a brain drain of the country's skilled and professional people. Frustrated by the rapidly deteriorating living standards and the poor conditions for creative work and research, over 450,000 Bulgarians have moved to developed countries such as Austria, Canada, France, Germany, and the United States. Most of these are young and well educated. Only some 60,000 of them are expected to return.

Today there are two main classes in Bulgarian society—the newly rich and the impoverished. The country needs a stable middle class, to secure its economic future and political stability. This class, however, has not as yet emerged.

DOCTORS DOING ODD JOBS

Class tensions are palpable in the country, especially since a number of the newly rich are former Communist officials. These former bureaucrats have made the most of their easy access to government resources during the recent years of transition to democracy.

This has led to the absurd situation in which intellectuals, academics, and professionals such as doctors have been forced to take on two or even three jobs in order to earn a decent living. As government employees, they receive such low salaries that they have little choice but to hold several jobs. More and more, money is linked to social prestige in a country where education used to matter most.

This man behind the camera may well be a government employee, forced to supplement his meager pay with a part-time job.

DRESSING UP

Bulgarians dress like most Westerners, and care about how they look. They like natural fabrics—cotton, wool, and silk—and they iron these devotedly. They tend to dress nicely even to go to the local store. A casual night out becomes an occasion to dress up.

Traditional Bulgarian clothes are richly ornamented, with bright, bold colors. Traditional styles usually included an embroidered vest that used to vary widely from region to region. Today these costumes are seen only on television or at village celebrations, and one can be certain that the brightly clad young men and women had rummaged in their grandparents' wardrobes.

Attention to clothing is a long-standing Bulgarian tradition. According to an old saying, "The greeting will measure how well you are dressed, the farewell will match how clever you have been."

A Bulgarian couple out strolling, with the man wearing a rather striking orange suit.

LIFESTYLE

THE MANY UPS AND DOWNS in the political life of the nation have taught Bulgarians to value a stable life among family and friends. They know that close relations can always be depended on—in moments of crisis, to help nurture the young, or to take care of the old.

In public places Bulgarians do not appear to be very welcoming. But once inside a Bulgarian home, that changes. It would be unheard of for a caller not to be offered a drink or a bite to eat, whether it is a friend who has dropped in casually, the mailperson, or a stranger.

Generally Bulgarians do not like the idea of letting the state take care of their loved ones in times of sickness or crisis. If possible, they prefer not to depend on hospitals, nursing homes, or banks. Your Bulgarian friends may never think of sending you Christmas or birthday cards, but in hard times they will offer their help even before you ask for it. In turn, they expect the same of you.

Opposite: **Art students have no scarcity of material to sketch in the old parts of Plovdiv.**

Below: **A favorite activity of older Bulgarians— chatting on a park bench.**

FEW MIXED MARRIAGES

Bulgarians tend to be strongly conservative in outlook. They do not approve of those who choose to remain single, and they frown upon couples who live together without getting married. A gay or lesbian partnership is quite incomprehensible to most Bulgarians.

Over 90% of the adult population of Bulgaria is married. Mixed marriages are virtually unknown in this overwhelmingly white society. Even different ethnic groups, or those with different religious backgrounds, do not intermarry. But friendships among all groups are encouraged or tolerated.

A stone relief of a close family unit, a venerated institution in Bulgaria.

THE FAMILY

The Bulgarian family often includes grandparents, aunts, uncles, and even cousins. Some Bulgarian homes have three or even four generations living together. This is partly due to the acute shortage of housing in the cities.

Bulgarians, traditionally a nation of small-scale farmers and artisans, do not resent sharing their homes with members of the extended family. Middle-aged or elderly parents are more likely to stay with a married daughter than with a married son.

The different generations under one roof usually get on well together. When two generations share a home, their roles are clearly defined. The younger people usually earn a living, and the older ones tend the home and help raise the children.

CLOSE TO THE GRANDPARENTS

Even when parents live away from their children, they often act as foster parents for their grandchildren during the summer months. First cousins, who frequently spend vacations together at their grandparents', may grow as close as brothers and sisters. Children often feel closer to their grandparents than to their parents, who are at work all day long and have the thankless task of being the disciplinarians.

The dream home of every Bulgarian is a multistoried house where parents and their children's families can each have their own floor, and "will not have to change shoes" to visit each other.

GRANDMOTHER'S DAY

January 21 is Grandmother's Day, one of the most touching Bulgarian holidays. It is also the professional holiday of obstetricians and gynaecologists. In the past, the oldest and most experienced woman in the family would help with the birth of her grandchildren.

Women today very rarely give birth at home, because trained medical professionals have displaced grandmothers from their function as midwives. But the grandmother's role in bringing up the young ones is still very much appreciated.

Grandmother's Day is a holiday for women. On this day Bulgarian women call on their grandmothers to wash their hands for them and to present them with a fluffy new towel. The same ritual is enacted in the maternity wards of hospitals—as an acknowledgment of the nurses' part in taking care of the mothers and their newborn.

A young couple in a public park. Bulgarians tend to marry early.

MARRIAGE AND DIVORCE

Bulgarians tend to marry for love. Often they get married before their careers are established and have little choice but to live with their parents. The high cost of housing means they are seldom able to move out of the parental home. Children are usually brought up by the extended family.

Except for the Muslim minorities, young couples have no more than two children. Stringent family planning is due both to tradition and to economic hardship. In marriage, both partners often preserve a significant degree of emotional and professional independence.

HERE COMES THE BRIDE Weddings traditionally take place in early spring or the fall. Preparations start months ahead, usually with the betrothal. In the city, betrothal typically takes place at a private party given by the immediate families of the couple. Presents are given, while the couple exchange rings—usually wedding bands that are worn on the left hand until the marriage, when they are shifted to the right hand. This is the time to settle issues of property and money. In the small villages, there may be a large feast to which the whole village is invited.

The wedding is a sumptuous affair, starting at dawn and often continuing overnight. During the wedding banquet, the mock complaint crops up repeatedly that the wine is bitter, and that the only way to "sweeten" the wine is by a passionate kiss of the newlyweds.

When a marriage fails to work, the partners are free to divorce. The court procedure, however, is long and complicated, giving the partners numerous options to reconsider their decision. Nevertheless, divorce rates are rising, especially in urban communities.

The children of divorced parents normally live with their mother until they come of age, when they can choose which parent they wish to live with. The father is usually given the right to spend weekends plus several weeks during vacations with his children. He is also required to pay some money for their support.

An Orthodox Christian wedding in church, performed by a priest.

Two Bulgarian women walking their dogs. They typify the fairly liberated lifestyle of females in the country. Women are integrated in all the social areas and have equal rights with men. Despite this, Bulgaria is no paradise for women. Family roles bear the mark of centuries of Islamic rule.

MEN AND WOMEN

Bulgarian women enjoy considerable freedom. This is the result of centuries of wars that took the men away from their families, leaving the women to act as providers.

Socialism has improved the quality of women's education, with laws passed for the equality of the sexes. State restrictions over earning potential had one effect beneficial to women. Families needed two substantial breadwinners, so women had little choice but to go out and work and excel in their jobs. Bulgarian women, who make up half the workforce, have proved to be talented politicians, professors, legislators, and administrators. Since 1989 Bulgaria has had its first woman vice-president and prime minister.

CHILDREN PLAY THEIR PART

Children are probably the most important members of Bulgarian society. Bulgarian parents will sacrifice anything for the well-being and the future of their children. A child's achievement is still a far greater source of family pride than material benefits or professional advancement.

Unless children happen to live with healthy and energetic grandparents, they learn to take care of themselves early. An older child, barely in his or her teens, will often prepare meals and set the table for the younger child and the grandparents. Bulgarian parents expect this and have a low tolerance for waywardness or misbehavior.

Most Bulgarian children remain dependent on their parents right into adulthood. But sooner or later, the roles are reversed, and the younger adults start to look after their aging parents. In this way, parents and children remain dependent on each other throughout their lives.

Two children perform in public to earn a bit of spare cash, either for pocket money or for their family.

MARRIED BUT STILL AT HOME It is considered a disgrace if a young adult leaves the parental home before marriage. Unless a promising career is at stake, the parents will be accused of having driven their child away.

Even after marriage, it is common for young couples to live with either set of parents. The young couple might help with utilities and other bills, but Bulgarians would not ask their children to pay rent. The parents would also contribute toward the new homes of their children and help with furnishings and decorations.

Students in class, looking a little tense. Most children their age start learning at least one foreign language.

PRIDE IN LEARNING

Bulgarians believe wholeheartedly in very few things, but they do believe in the value of education. The Bulgarian educational system is comprehensive and very stringent, with unique opportunities for study. Competitive exams regulate access to education. The demand for good education at all levels is so high that even some of the new private schools, where students pay high tuition fees, have introduced entrance exams.

Bulgarian education has a long democratic tradition. From the National Revival period of the 19th century onward, Bulgarians have taken pride in supporting their schools. Small mountain villages used to pool together their resources to send their most talented youths to prestigious schools in the cities or even abroad.

In Bulgaria school attendance is compulsory and free. Because of a "tracking" system, the high school dropout levels are very low. Students of lower academic potential enroll in vocational schools, where the emphasis is on practical training for a trade.

Between the ages of 6–7 and 9–10, children attend elementary school. At the junior-high level, between the ages of 9–10 and 13–14, most children start learning at least one foreign language. This is when students are introduced to the basic humanities and sciences. After the seventh or eighth grade, they face a major decision. They have to choose their high school, apply to get in, and may have to take an entrance exam.

There are two main types of high school in Bulgaria. Vocational schools offer three years of practical training in industry, transportation, agriculture, or commerce. A student with a degree from such a school cannot pursue higher education. All other high schools enable students to move on to higher education upon graduation. For adolescents with special talents, a number of high schools provide intensive advanced education in the arts, languages, or mathematics. Colleges and universities train specialists for the professional job market.

Two college students on a visit to Bachkovo monastery.

UNIVERSITIES IN SHAKE-UP

Until recently the numbers of college graduates were regulated through centralized planning. Admission standards were very stringent, and only the best students were taken in, without having to pay fees.

The university system in Bulgaria is undergoing reform. Private colleges have started up, charging fees but offering more flexible programs. Public universities now make certain candidates pay, namely those who have passed the entrance exam but have not made it to the top of the admissions list.

All the same, a proposal to introduce tuition fees for all universities provoked outrage among a wide section of Bulgarian society. Bulgarians firmly believe in the availability of education to everyone.

FRIENDS AND STRANGERS

It is hard being a stranger in Bulgarian society. Even in a small village, strangers get only a hesitant "hello," and only after the elderly people, seated on the benches in front of their homes, have looked them up and down. In the cities people ignore each other. Office clerks and shop assistants appear to wear stone masks.

Strolling in the afternoon sun after a visit to a café or a restaurant is a popular activity.

On the other hand, Bulgarians are kind and generous to anybody who enters their homes. There is a moving Christmas tradition that speaks volumes for Bulgarian hospitality. The woman of the house brings out the Christmas pie stuck with little dogwood twigs that are to tell each family member their luck for the coming year. But before she serves the pie, the hostess sets aside a piece for "Grandpa Vassil"—the stranger who has not managed to make it home through the snow-covered country roads.

HOUSE AND GARDEN Except for the biggest cities, life in urban and rural areas is fairly similar. There are libraries, youth clubs, entertainment complexes, and attractive restaurants in all the small towns and the villages. Most homes are occupied by one or two families, with front yards planted with flowers and with neat vegetable plots in the back.

Bulgarians are fond of their gardens. Whether they have to travel to the outskirts of the city to tend their plot, or merely step out into their backyard, Bulgarians cultivate their garden plots to perfection.

Thriving villages, especially those in the mountains in the southcentral and southeastern parts of the country, became almost depopulated when people started moving to the cities to work during the industrialization period. The cities, on the other hand, experienced severe housing shortages. To cope with this, the government started subsidizing housing projects. Today most of the population in the large cities live in these hastily built and unattractive buildings.

LEAVING FOR THE COUNTRYSIDE Driven by the current economic crisis, experienced most acutely in the industrial sector, families are now beginning to leave the big cities. Life in the countryside is cheaper, less stressful, healthier, and there are more local possibilities for enterprising individuals. As a result the Bulgarian villages and small towns are once again coming back to life.

Cities are meanwhile witnessing the rebirth of the one-family home. New Bulgarian houses are solid and beautiful, with deep foundations, brick walls, and red-tiled roofs. When they build a home, Bulgarians plan it so that a new floor for a future generation can be added on.

RELIGION

SEVERAL RELIGIONS ARE PRACTICED in Bulgaria, but none very fervently. The 1992 census showed that nearly 86% of the population think of themselves as Orthodox Christians. That is, they follow the kind of Christianity prevalent today in Greece, Romania, Serbia, Macedonia, Syria, Georgia, and in parts of Finland, Poland, the Czech Republic, Slovakia, Hungary, and Croatia.

Another 13% define themselves as Muslims, 0.6% are Roman Catholic, and 0.2% are Protestant.

These figures represent an overwhelming number of believers, considering that less than a decade ago Bulgarians were described as atheist. But few Bulgarian Orthodox Christians have a clear understanding of the meaning of their faith. Their religion is largely a matter of tradition and a symbol of their loyalty to the nation.

FAITH AND POLITICS

During the Communist era, the Orthodox Church was pushed to the margins of social life. Religious knowledge was no longer part of the state educational system. The church was banned from its traditional activities, such as running orphanages and hospitals. Religious holidays and the rites of baptism, marriage, and burial were replaced by socialist holidays and rituals.

The constitution of 1971 guaranteed freedom of religious beliefs and rituals, but the state made it very clear to all students and government employees that attending religious services would damage their future and their careers.

Above: **Shipka church, a monument to the victory of the Liberation War (1877–1878).**

Opposite: **An Orthodox Christian priest stands beneath the painted ceiling of Bachkovo monastery.**

ORTHODOX CHRISTIANITY

Religious knowledge had been commonly passed on from one generation to another. But this source was cut off after industrialization in the 1960s and 1970s brought a lot of young people from the villages into the cities. The constitution of 1971 also required parents to give their children a "Communist upbringing," and it stipulated that the education of youth "in a Communist spirit is the duty of the entire society."

Politicians hold a rally, with a strong presence of priests.

A RESURGENCE The sustained efforts of the state to inculcate an atheist way of life were largely successful. The changes that began in 1989 affected the place of the Orthodox Church in the life of the people. It was no coincidence that the huge rallies of the anti-Communist opposition were held in the squares in front of city cathedrals. This choice of venue meant that once again, the democratic movement was symbolically connected to the Orthodox Church.

For many centuries the Orthodox Church was virtually unknown in the Western world. Although there have been numerous contacts between the Orthodox, Catholic, and Reformed Churches recently, the differences among them are still not clear to many people. In both the East and the West, Christians believe in the Holy Trinity of Christ, the Father and the Holy Spirit, and base their belief on the Old and New Testaments.

Rallies held in front of cathedral squares were meant to relay the message that once again, the church was to be part of political life.

HEART OF THE CONTROVERSY

The churches of the East and the West differ on certain controversial points. These are the same ones encountered by the Church fathers when spreading Christianity in the early centuries of the faith. Eastern theology upholds the absolute equality of the Son, the Father, and the Holy Spirit, and that each entity is different in relation to the other. Western theology, on the other hand, emphasizes the unity of God, and that the Holy Spirit proceeds from the Father just as from the Son.

The heart of the controversy between the two churches concerns the administrative hierarchy. The Western side has a monarchical conception of the Church, in which the Pope has right of rule over the whole of Christendom. The Eastern side sees Christendom as a community of self-governing churches, without needing to recognize papal supremacy.

ROLE OF THE CHURCH

The Orthodox Church has played an important role in the building and survival of the Bulgarian nation. The Slavs and the Bulgars who founded the Bulgarian state in A.D. 681 had quite different belief systems, which presented obstacles to their integration. Each of these peoples believed in a pantheon of deities ruled by a mighty God of Thunder—called Perun by the Slavic tribes, and Tangra by the Bulgars.

Bulgaria was converted to Christianity by Byzantine priests in the ninth century. Ever since, the Bulgarians have insisted on having their own national church, on a par with Constantinople's.

The changes in the practices of the Eastern Church in Bulgaria, brought about by the two theologians Cyril and Methodius, prevented cultural assimilation by the Byzantine empire. In their everyday teachings, Cyril and Methodius used the common spoken Slavic language and as well as their own Slavic translations of the Scriptures, written in the new Cyrillic alphabet.

After the fall of Bulgaria to the Turks, the independent Bulgarian Church came under the authority of the Greek Patriarch in Constantinople. The National Revival movement, which gave the nation back its place in history, started as a movement within the Church. This movement gathered pace after the passionate assertion of Bulgarian historical identity by Father Paisii, a monk from the Chilendar monastery, in his *Slav-Bulgarian History*.

The first independent Bulgarian schools were opened in the monasteries. In 1870 the Turkish sultan issued a decree granting Bulgarians the right to organize a Bulgarian Orthodox Church. As the first Bulgarian national institution in the Ottoman empire, the Orthodox Church played an important role in the movement for national liberation.

THE BOGOMIL INFLUENCE ON RELIGION

One of the most popular Christian movements was started in the 10th century by the Bogomils and spread quickly into Asia Minor, Serbia, and Bosnia. The movement deeply influenced medieval religious groups in Central and Western Europe—the Cathari in Italy, the Albigenses in France, and the Hussites in Bohemia (today's Czech Republic).

Named after its founder, Father Bogomil, the movement was directed against "earthly rulers and injustices," namely the feudal lords, the official church, and the king. It was born out of the despair of the peasantry, for the successors of Tzar Simeon had plunged the country into political and social disarray.

The Bogomils believed that the physical world was the creation of the Devil. They lived in communes of believers and practiced strict sexual abstinence. They proclaimed direct communion between the believer and God, honored neither the cross nor the icons, and fiercely attacked the social and political order in medieval Bulgaria. They were persecuted by the state, but survived as a movement for several centuries.

REVIVAL OF RELIGIOUS LIFE

A revival of religious life has been taking place in Bulgaria since the emergence of democracy in 1989. But the Bulgarian Orthodox Church as an institution is in deep crisis. The Communist regime is partly to blame, having severely discouraged those with a religious vocation.

With 2,500 functioning Orthodox churches in the country, there are only about 800 priests to perform church services, half of whom are due to retire. There has also been a split between church leaders who came to power in the Communist era and the younger religious leaders of the democratic movement.

The newer group wants a change, and accuse the older church leaders of corruption and the promotion of Communist interests. But this group is in turn accused of blindly serving political powers.

A river baptism in a small town, a testimony to the upsurge of religious feelings in the country.

FOUR MUSLIM GROUPS

After Orthodox Christianity, Islam has the second largest number of followers in Bulgaria. There are four Muslim groups in Bulgaria—Turks, Pomaks, Muslim Gypsies, and Tartars.

With very few exceptions, the Bulgarian Muslims are Sunnis. Traditionally living in close communities and isolated from the life of other Bulgarians, they maintain a strong sense of ethnic and religious identity. But few Muslims, whether of Turkish or Bulgarian origin, show a strong attachment to secular Turkey.

Like the Orthodox Christians, all Muslim communities in Bulgaria had an impoverished religious life under the Communist regime. It was far more severe for the Muslims, since they were under intense pressure to abandon their faith and to assimilate.

The Turks were consistently thinned out by emigration, resulting in a steep drop in the number of imams—the prayer leaders of the mosques.

A mosque in a busy part of Sofia. Bulgarian Muslims are devout in their faith.

ISLAM AND OTHER FAITHS

MUSLIMS During the Communist era, mosques rapidly disappeared from the Muslim villages, with modern buildings taking their place. Pilgrimages to Mecca, one of the Five Pillars of Islam, became practically impossible. A general ignorance of the tenets of Islam, including the Five Pillars, was the result. The Islamic Institute in Sofia started training religious leaders in 1989, but the current state of Islam in the country is none too bright.

JEWS The Jews in Bulgaria were a well-organized religious community until World War II. Most of them are Sephardics (Ladino-speaking), who arrived from Spain, but there are also some Ashkenasics (Yiddish-speaking), who came from countries north of the Danube. The Jews were governed by a central consistory (church council) and a chief rabbi in Sofia. Cities with a large concentration of Jews had their own consistory and rabbi.

After the establishment of the state of Israel, a mass exodus in 1948–1949 left behind only about 6,000 Jews, most of them in Sofia and largely nonbelievers. Today only the synagogues in Sofia, Samokov, and Vidin are occasionally open. There are no rabbis and only one cantor (synagogue official) in Sofia.

OTHER CHRISTIANS The 22,000 Bulgarian Armenians are mostly descendants of refugees from the persecution of Armenians in Turkey. They are adherents of the Armenian Gregorian Church. In religious affairs they are headed by an Armenian

A Baptist pastor giving a sermon.

Gregorian bishop who resides in Bucharest, Romania. The Armenian Church maintains close contacts with the Bulgarian Orthodox Church.

The Bulgarian Catholics have a complex history that dates back to the 13th and 14th centuries when Franciscan missionaries established communities in western Bulgaria.

The Protestant community is the smallest Christian group and the one with the most recent history. The first converts were made in the mid-19th century by American Methodist and Congregationalist missionaries in southern Bulgaria.

Both Catholics and Protestants received harsh treatment during the years of the Cold War, allegedly because of their ties with "hostile foreign centers" in the West. Pastors, priests, nuns, and lay believers were charged with spying for the West and anti-Communist propaganda. But there has been a marked revival among these religious groups since the 1970s.

LANGUAGE

TO BULGARIAN POETS, their language is sacred, as it has played an important role in preserving national identity. It belongs to the Southern Slavic group of languages, along with Macedonian, Serbian, and Croatian. Fewer than 20 words can be traced back to the tongue of the ancient Bulgars, which is believed to have been of Turanian origin.

The main languages spoken in Bulgaria are Bulgarian, Turkish, Armenian, and Greek.

BULGARIAN has absorbed many Turkish words, as well as grammatical features of other non-Slavic Balkan languages. It is the official language spoken by all citizens, although their mother tongue may be different, such as Turkish or Armenian.

Above: **A man holds up a newspaper. Beside him is a church billboard.**

Opposite: **A "museum" of Communist propaganda, derided as trash by demonstrators who had put it on display during the summer of 1990.**

TURKISH is spoken by many Muslims in the southcentral and northeastern parts of Bulgaria. It is a Turanian language related to the tongue of the old Bulgars, but very different from modern Bulgarian. The Muslims originated from the same parts of Central Asia that were home to the Turkish conquerors of the Bulgarian kingdom in the 14th century.

ARMENIAN is an Indo-European language spoken by the descendants of the Armenian holocaust refugees. In the early 20th century Armenians settled in Bulgaria east of the Black Sea. Over four million people in the former Soviet Union, Iraq, Lebanon, Syria, Iran, and Turkey speak this exotic language, which has its own alphabet.

GREEK is spoken by Bulgarian Greeks along the Black Sea coast and in the south of the country. It is written in a unique script, the basis for the Cyrillic alphabet used in Bulgaria, Macedonia, and Russia.

THE SLAVIC INHERITANCE

Signs outside a coffee house are in Bulgarian, but one of them has included an English word "kiwi."

The Bulgarians are justly proud of their language. They were the first among the Slavic peoples to create a rich religious and secular literature. And it was the Slavic brothers Cyril and Methodius whom the whole of Medieval Europe had to thank for the Cyrillic script. Their invention of Slavic letters and translation of the Scriptures into the spoken Slavic language was an outstanding cultural achievement.

Cyril and Methodius had originally devised the Slav-Bulgarian alphabet for the purpose of establishing a Slavic church in Moravia (present-day Slovakia). The church mission collapsed and the alphabet system would have disappeared along with it—except that some of the disciples of the Slavic apostles found refuge in Bulgaria.

The educational and creative work of these disciples issued in a Golden Age of literature and culture in their new country. In the churches and at court, the Bulgarian language replaced Greek. The Cyrillic alphabet, along with Slavic liturgy, literature, and law, spread from Bulgaria to Serbia, Russia, and other lands.

Bulgarian became the international language of Slavic civilization, carrying cultural accomplishments and influences throughout the Balkans and northward to Russia. A number of Slavic peoples still use the Cyrillic script, with some minor variations to accommodate phonetic differences.

Bulgarian has an alphabet of 30 letters, with six vowels, two letters for composite diphthongs, 20 consonants, and two letters to indicate short vowels or soft consonants. It is a melodious language, not difficult to

pronounce, but with an extremely complicated grammar. Although Bulgaria is a small country, there are considerable regional differences among the dialects spoken. These concern mainly the sound of words, but there are also Bulgarian dialects with variations in word choice, and even some grammatical differences.

CYRIL AND METHODIUS: APOSTLES OF THE SLAVS

The Slav brothers Cyril and Methodius were experienced missionaries and brilliant church intellectuals. The younger brother, Constantine the Philosopher, whose monastic name was Cyril, was educated at the school for the children of the Byzantine imperial family. He had a gift for languages and held prestigious positions as professor of philosophy at the Magnaura Palace School and as librarian of the patriarchal church of St. Sophia in Constantinople.

In their missionary and translating work, and as inventors of the script, the brothers worked wholeheartedly for the enlightenment of the Slavs. They bravely defended their cause in the home of their adversaries—the Holy City of Rome. But their work among the Slavs of Moravia antagonized the German clergy who regarded Moravia as their missionary field. The two brothers were accused of heresy for not teaching Christianity in one of the three holy languages—Greek, Latin, or Hebrew.

They were summoned by the Pope to account for their actions. On their way to Rome they were drawn into a dispute with Venetian clergymen. It was here that Cyril formulated his defense of the use of the Slavic language in liturgy and learning.

Three young men in conversation outside a café, one of them giving the photographer the universal peace sign.

BODY LANGUAGE

Bulgarians may appear somewhat reserved, yet they often become very animated during conversations. They use their eyes, eyebrows, and hands to emphasize a point or to express approval or disagreement. When speaking, both men and women tend to touch each other much more often than people in most Western cultures. They also stand closer together and converse in louder voices.

Perhaps most confusing is the habit of shaking the head to express agreement or compliance. It thus appears to others that Bulgarians are always disagreeing with each other. What is more, a Bulgarian gently nods his head to signify "no," though this is more easily understood by an accompanying series of clicking sounds of the tongue. To confuse matters, there are Bulgarians who shake and nod their heads in the Western manner. On top of all this, the Greek minority shares with Bulgarians the same gestures for "yes" and "no," but the Greek word for "no" means "yes" in Bulgarian.

Bulgarians greet each other very warmly. It is common among members of both sexes to extend one or both hands to each other, and to exchange two or three kisses on the cheek (even numbers are considered bad luck). One can often see couples, even of the same sex, walking with arms intertwined. This is not necessarily a sign of affection, but rather of trust and deep engagement in conversation. Similarly, a waving finger may not signify a threat, but may merely draw attention to a point of importance. Actual disapproval is easily inferred from a series of loud clicking sounds and from raised eyebrows.

One place in Bulgaria where strangers might begin a conversation or even offer each other a drink is the train compartment.

CONVERSATIONS ON THE TRAIN

Nearly everyone in Bulgaria travels on a train at some time during the year. College students and professors, retirees and professionals, soldiers, the unemployed, commuters, and vacationers all travel by train. As a result, a lively cross section of Bulgarian society can be encountered on a journey.

A train is hardly out of the station when someone will start to talk—perhaps exclaiming about a newspaper article. Another passenger may take out a homemade pie, and someone else may offer some fresh fruit or a drink.

The train is the place to hear the funniest and the most heartbreaking life stories and to share in the happiness, aspirations, love, or tragedy of total strangers. Bulgarians do not hesitate to ask pointed questions about one's marriage, age, professional status, or salary. Two or more conversations can take place simultaneously in one train compartment. By the end of the journey, strangers who would not have looked at each other on a bus or in a café part like friends.

Students are polite to teachers, taking care to address them formally even when they have left school or college and become friends with former tutors.

NAMES AND FORMS OF ADDRESS

Bulgarians have three names—the given name, the father's name, and the family name, which can sometimes be the paternal grandfather's name. It is a common tradition to call children after their grandparents, and so the given name of the firstborn son differs from the family name only in its ending. For example, Georgi Georgiev, meaning Georgi's Georgi.

Variations on the grandparents' names are frequent. These may keep only the root or just a recognizable cluster of sounds—as in the case of Ralitza, named after the girl's grandmother Radka; or as in Miloslav, after grandfather Milko.

The family name is the usual form of address at work, preceded by a polite Mr., Mrs., Miss, Doctor, or Professor. Sometimes people prefer to use their father's name. This is an especially common choice among young professional women who have embarked on a career before marriage. It is a way of acknowledging the father's financial and moral support through college.

When Bulgarians talk to strangers, they invariably use the polite form of address. The formal "you" is appropriate for addressing business associates, unless there is a close working relationship. This is also the mandatory form of addressing one's teachers and professors, even when students and teachers have become friends in adulthood.

When a Bulgarian woman marries, she can adopt her husband's last name, retain her old family name, or combine the two in hyphenated form. Women who marry young usually opt for the traditional choice of adopting the husband's name. But female college graduates now prefer to retain their family name after marriage, or at least some form of it.

Names, especially last names, can indicate the person's ethnic origin. Typically, last names have Slavic endings, except for some Jewish and Armenian names. Thus the family name derived from the Greek name Stavros has the masculine form of Stavrev and the feminine form of Stavreva.

No Slavic endings are added to the Jewish family name Grinberg, for example, or to the Armenian Vartanyan.

The informal "you" form of addressing someone is reserved for conversations with close friends, family, and children.

These Bulgarian women are likely to have adopted their husband's name, unlike young female graduates who are opting increasingly to keep their own family name.

ARTS

THE ARTS IN BULGARIA have a long history, dating back to ancient times. The Thracians, Romans, ancient Greeks, Bulgars, and medieval Bulgarians have all left traces of their unique artistic life. Every year archeologists and historians uncover some artistic monument of the past. Tombs with exquisite frescoes and silver and golden treasures have been unearthed. So have Roman baths with mosaics, amphitheaters, statues, and illuminated manuscripts.

A distinctive feature of the Bulgarian arts is their strong democratic tradition. Long centuries of foreign rule prevented the high art forms from developing, as these were traditionally sponsored by the state.

The political ups and downs of the nation have also influenced the Bulgarian visual arts, theater, and literature. Bulgaria has few imposing medieval fortresses or cathedrals, no courtly literature, and no chamber music tradition.

FOLK MUSIC AND DANCE

What it does have is a rich regional variety of folk music and dance, fine examples of handicrafts, interesting architectural and interior design, icons and church frescoes, and a tradition of local centers of cultural life.

Bulgarian folk music is popular worldwide. It has varied meters, lively rhythms, and an irregular beat. Folk songs tell of the joy of work, of inconsolable grief for lost children, of legendary and heroic figures who protected the people from foreign invaders, and of the people's longing for freedom.

Above: **Icon paintings in Shipka church.**

Opposite: **Architectural detail from the 14th century church of Christ the Pantocrator in Nessebar.**

BAGPIPES AND SAD SONGS

Bulgarian folk songs vary dramatically from region to region. In the Rhodope, they tend to be slow and sad, sung to the accompaniment of low-pitched bagpipes. In the Sofia region the rhythm picks up, resulting in wild, fast tunes. In the Pirin the complex harmonies of the songs rise to unimaginably high pitches.

Closely related to the musical folklore tradition are the folk dances of Bulgaria. The best known of these is the *horo* ("ho-RO"), a lively circular dance where the dancers hold hands and swirl round to the wild rhythm of the music. This dance is popular in many parts of Bulgaria.

Also well-liked is the *ruchenitza* ("rah-che-NI-tza"), a competitive dance where the best dancers in the village, men against women, challenge each other's stamina and imagination.

GIFT OF THE FIRE DANCERS

In the secluded hills of the Strandja Mountains, one can witness an unforgettable dance of very ancient origin. On May 21, the day of the two saints Constantine and Helena, the local people light huge bonfires. At sunset, when the fires have turned to red-hot embers, the dances begin, to the beat of drums. Barefoot men and women, carrying old icons in their hands, start to circle round the embers, picking up the fast drum rhythm. Then, raising the icons high above their heads, they step into the fire. The dance is long and ecstatic. At the end, the dancers shake the ashes and the embers from their feet and step out on to the grass—quite unharmed. Nobody remembers any of them ever suffering from burns or scorches.

These dancers are called the Nestinari. Their talent is handed down from generation to generation in certain families. And even then, not every family member has the gift. Those who do, tell of how they cannot resist an inner call to perform the dance.

The folk traditions in music and dance date back to the long centuries of Ottoman rule, but they are very much alive today. Bulgarians love to sing and perform on festive occasions.

The country has several professional ensembles for folk music and dancing, which bring these unique art forms to world audiences. A number of Bulgarian composers, both new and old, have been influenced by Bulgarian folk tunes and have used them in their works.

Male dancers like to challenge the women in competitive dancing.

BULGARIAN CHURCH ART

Little remains of the earliest medieval art of the Bulgarian churches, but what has been preserved is striking. One well-known example is a ninth century ceramic icon of St. Theodore, which invites comparison with the art of Egypt and of the Syria-Palestine region.

Some ceramic fragments from church decorations in Preslav feature pictures of saints and archangels together with lions and monkeys. There are also the larger-than-life, earthy paintings from the Second Bulgarian Kingdom, found in the Boyana church near Sofia and in the cave church near Ivanovo village. in the Ruse district.

Most Bulgarian icons date from the Ottoman period when Christianity, once the stronghold of state power, became the faith of the "insulted and the injured," as in its early days. These icons are often austere and mystical stylizations, rendered in both vibrant and dark colors.

The Bulgarian icon became more expressive during the National Revival period. Its distinctive features include an interest in human personality, dramatic detail, and landscape elements.

Icon painters, goldsmiths, woodcarvers, and other artisans blended Islamic art with Western European styles and the Balkan art of icon-making. They developed their own schools, each with a distinctive style. The religious art of the 18th and 19th centuries expressed a marked confidence in artistry.

ZOGRAPH: ICON PAINTER OF VISION

Zakhari Zograph was one of the most talented and ambitious painters from the Samokov school of iconographers in the 19th century. He came from an artistic family—a brother of his painted the scenes of the Apocalypse in Rila monastery.

Zograph had no formal art education in the European schools, but he studied Western engravings and paintings in his father's collection. His frescoes adorn the walls of dozens of Bulgarian churches. He seemed to be spurred on by the image of the wheel of life, which he painted in the monasteries of Preobrazhenie and Troyan. He was consumed by an urge to fulfill his creative potential before the wheel lowered him into the open jaws of the monster in his painting.

The frescoes of Zograph illustrate dramatic Biblical scenes, but they also depict the ordinary lives of people of the Bulgarian towns and villages. The highest compliment to his talent was an invitation to paint in the cathedral church on holy Mount Athos. This was a recognition that the artist from Samokov had no rival in the whole of the Turkish empire.

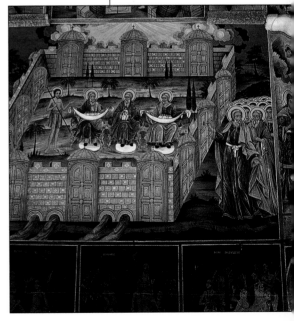

A vibrant example of mural painting in the open gallery of the church of Rila monastery.

PRIESTS AND POETS

From its Golden Age to the present, the literature of the Bulgarian people has been linked with the political life of the nation. The first generation of medieval Bulgarian writers broke down the dogma of the three holy languages of Christianity—Hebrew, Greek, and Latin.

The beginning of the National Revival period was marked by Father Paisii's *Slav-Bulgarian History*, which was to become a gospel for the Bulgarian Enlightenment. Hristo Botev, a fiery fighter for national liberation, was also a poet of rare talent and a perceptive journalist. The verses of Geo Milev were deemed such a powerful weapon that he was executed.

More recently the death-knell for the Communist regime was sounded by the new generation of Bulgarian writers and poets, who were fearless in their condemnation of state corruption and mediocrity.

ART OF SATIRE

Bulgaria has a strong theatrical tradition, alive to the political pulse of the nation. The first theatrical performances in Bulgaria took place on the stages of the popular library clubs during the middle of the last century. They were organized by schoolteachers and educators, and were intended to stir national consciousness and spur the people on to fight for independence and social justice.

The first whiff of the liberating spirit of perestroika in Bulgaria came from the theater and the cinema. Playwrights, scriptwriters, and film producers worked out a symbolic language, which eluded government censorship. Their works, complete with philosophic and moral parables, allowed them to launch attacks on the regime of the day—in the form of bitter political satires. The cinemas and theaters of Bulgaria became the first zones where government propaganda gave way to free thinking.

IMPOSSIBLE ACTS

Between 1977 and 1981, the Ministry of Culture was headed by Lyudmila Zhivkova, daughter of the long-reigning dictator Todor Zhivkov. This was a "pseudo-Golden Age" of Bulgarian art, when state support was exceptionally generous, but artistic production was tightly controlled, with severe penalties for transgression.

In the 1980s cultural funding from the state began dwindling until it practically stopped. Suddenly freed from the censorship mechanism, but with no financial support, Bulgarian artists started forming small groups to share production costs. Groups such as the Society for Art in Action and the City Group came into being.

This new generation of artists is willing to experiment and to be politically involved—they work with unconventional materials, exhibit in unusual places, and integrate exhibition with performance.

The Bulgarian cinema and theater are not faring so well. Left without state support after the fall of Socialist rule, the entire film industry all but collapsed. The number of new productions dropped drastically, film-making technicians lost their jobs in droves, and cinemas and theaters started closing down. The theaters have a higher survival rate, but they have also edged close to bankruptcy.

Forced against the wall, the Bulgarian theater and cinema are coming up with works of fervent spiritual intensity. Directors and casts are striving to respond to popular demand, but the emphasis is still on moral and artistic responsibility, rather than on entertainment.

A cinema in Plovdiv, showing both Bulgarian and Western films.

Some of the discoveries of Bulgarian archeologists have been exhibited in countries all over the world.

ANCIENT DIGS

Bulgaria is a paradise for archeologists. Because it is the site of several ancient civilizations, excavations are taking place all the time—in the countryside, in Bulgarian cities that rest on ancient foundations, and even in the coastal waters of the Black Sea.

KAZANLUK TOMB Two thousand years ago the thriving civilization of the Thracians was subdued by the Roman legions. The tomb of a Thracian tribal chief, built in the third century B.C., was discovered in 1944 in the city of Kazanluk. The man was buried along with all the finery and decorated weapons that he might need in the afterlife.

The craftsmanship of the Thracian masters is especially evident in the perfectly preserved frescoes. Human and animal figures, painted in vibrant colors, look as if they are about to step off the wall. The chief and his wife are portrayed as touching each other tenderly.

PLOVDIV AMPHITHEATER People hardly dare dig foundations for new buildings in the center of Plovdiv in case they damage valuable ancient monuments. One such rare find, on the side of the Old Town, is a huge amphitheater, dating back to Roman times. The structure was found to be perfectly preserved—from the stage to the most distant row of seats. Today Bulgarians can enjoy a play in this amphitheater, under the summer sky, overlooking the historical hills of ancient Plovdiv.

The Roman amphitheater in Plovdiv, where drama companies like to stage their plays.

LEISURE

BACK FROM A DAY'S WORK, Bulgarians do not kick off their shoes and relax. Instead they promptly busy themselves with tasks around the house. In the words of an old Bulgarian saying, "It's fine to work in vain, but not to sit around in vain." Later in the evening they prefer to read, whether books or newspapers, than to watch television.

When Bulgarian women get together, they are likely to bring some work along with them. A leisurely afternoon with friends can involve helping each other with a knitting or embroidery project. Or they may help with the cooking for a forthcoming celebration.

The leisure pursuits of the men traditionally include making wine and local brandy. Bulgarians are convinced that there is no better wine than their own, produced from grapes and fruits of their own labors.

Left: **A relaxing hour knitting on the front porch. Bulgarian women are fond of spending their leisure time doing some sort of handiwork.**

Opposite: **Bulgarians love to read in their spare time. Newspapers, in the current climate of democratic reform, are eagerly scanned.**

WEEKEND ACTIVITIES

Making wine is a favorite weekend communal activity in the fall. Friends rally round to help, taste each other's produce, tell stories, and sing songs. The men may also indulge in a game of cards or backgammon.

Gardening is another popular weekend pursuit. This is a hobby, rather than work. Those in small towns and villages have little gardens in their backyards, and those in the cities travel to the outskirts or to summer houses in the countryside to tend their plots.

Bulgarians are perfectionists when it comes to gardening. Along the Black Sea coast, little family vineyards get just as much attention.

Bulgarian men play a game of backgammon.

COFFEE, COFFEE EVERYWHERE

Bulgarians drink coffee at all hours of the day, and especially in the late afternoon. At the weekend and in July and August city dwellers stroll along streets dotted with dozens of small cafés, each with its own distinct atmosphere and a faithful clientele.

Some of the cafés are like social clubs, where lawyers, actors, university professors, writers, artists, and those in the film industry each have their chosen corner.

Next to dropping in at a coffee house, Bulgarians love to visit friends and relatives. They bring flowers and perhaps a bottle of homemade wine. But these days, because of their busy lifestyle, it is usually some special occasion that brings them knocking on someone's door.

Apart from public holidays, important days are birthdays and name days—the days devoted to patron saints in the Eastern Orthodox Christian calendar. It is a mark of social prestige to be remembered by a lot of people on this day.

Coffee houses are favorite places for relaxing, exchanging news, and renewing friendships and old contacts. For decades, cafés in Bulgarian cities have been magnets for professionals, students, and retirees.

A typical scene on the beach in summer. Young Bulgarians flock to the Black Sea coast whenever they can.

TO THE BEACH AND MOUNTAINS

In July and August most Bulgarians leave town for their vacation. The theaters and concert halls close for the summer, the cities grow hot and dusty, and school is out. Families with relatives in the countryside visit and help with the fieldwork.

The most popular vacationing places remain the mountains and the Black Sea coast. Their numerous resorts offer facilities such as camping sites, shelters, and chalets for people of all tastes and incomes.

The Black Sea coast, with its warm clear water and sandy beaches, with adjacent forests and river deltas and spectacular vegetation, is by far the best loved vacation area for most Bulgarians. They come here to relax, camp, swim, fish, and row. Those who live by the sea usually spend their vacations in the mountains—green and cool, with crystal clear lakes, modern resorts, and well marked hiking routes.

FAVORITE SPORTS

The Bulgarian mountains are also popular in the winter months. The biggest mountain resorts are in the Rila mountains, the Rhodope, and Mount Vitosha. Good snowfalls and snow cover that lasts up to 180 days of the year make for excellent skiing conditions.

The young people of Bulgaria enjoy skiing, especially those from

Men and women doing outdoor aerobics.

Sofia. The city is located at the foot of Mount Vitosha, only a half-hour drive from excellent ski and toboggan runs.

Other sports loved by Bulgarian youngsters are soccer and basketball. Little boys, whether from a city or a small village, learn to kick a soccer ball almost as soon as they can walk. Soccer games are always well attended. The country's soccer players are highly popular celebrities. When the Bulgarian soccer team defeated the might of Germany in the quarterfinals of the 1994 World Cup, the response back in Bulgaria was tremendous, and a spectacular rally was held in Sofia.

Basketball, a recent arrival in the country, is more popular in the cities. Schoolchildren, both girls and boys, play this game.

Other favorites include volleyball, rowing, rhythm gymnastics, track events, wrestling, and weightlifting. Generations of Bulgarians have excelled at these sports in international competitions.

LAUGHING IT OFF

When things get tough for the Bulgarians, they respond by an avalanche of jokes, perhaps over a game of cards or a short coffee break. Jokes also liven up family dinners. Bulgarians are especially good at making fun of what scares and upsets them but what they have no power to change.

NEWSPAPERS AND NOVELS

Bulgarians love to read. The daily newspapers became everybody's favorite reading material for about two years after democratic changes began. At the time it was very difficult to get hold of a leading newspaper after 8 a.m. This hunger for real political news, however, has now been met, and Bulgarians have gone back to their usual fare—novels, short fiction, and poetry. Bulgarians have remained faithful to the book. They read everywhere—on the train, on the bus, or at home in the evenings. Public libraries and bookstores are always full of people. When the weather is fine, book vendors are out in the city centers, with small crowds of readers sampling their wares.

GABROVO: HOME OF HUMOR AND SATIRE

There is a city in Bulgaria which has an international reputation for laughing at its own citizens. This is Gabrovo, an important industrial center in the heart of Bulgaria. It boasts the world's first Home of Humor and Satire, which opened in 1974.

The world's only Festival of Humor and Satire started in Gabrovo in 1965 and has been held there every year since. "The world," the people of Gabrovo say, "has survived because it has laughed."

Here are a few typical jokes and anecdotes that poke fun at the slyness and stinginess of Gabrovo's citizens:

A young man told his father he wanted to become a doctor—a heart specialist. "You fool!" said his father. "Better study dentistry. Man has got one heart, but 32 teeth."

Two Gabrovo drivers met on a narrow bridge, but neither would go back, in order to save fuel. One took out a newspaper and began to read, thinking the other would soon get fed up and back up. But the other driver got out, sat down on the hood of his car and said, "After you've read the paper, can I borrow it?"

When entertaining guests on a name day, Gabrovo citizens put two or three cracked nuts on top of a heap of nutshells, for the sake of economy and in order to let people think that many guests have visited the name-day celebrant.

When renting rooms, they always make sure that they get a window near a lamp post.

The most popular jokes put their finger on the shortcomings of the Bulgarian's national character, or on the inadequacies of ruling politicians.

FUNNY STORIES

It was at the turn of the century that journalist and nature-lover Aleko Konstantinov created the character of Bai Ganyu that has brought so many smiles to the faces of the normally serious Bulgarians.

Bulgarians are fond of telling stories. Their favorite characters are sly peasants, not too polished, but daring and witty. Two such enduring figures are Sly Peter, who was created 1,300 years ago, and Bai Ganyu, who made his first appearance in 1895.

There is no Bulgarian who has not chuckled over the adventures of these two comic characters. Sly Peter is adept at outwitting everybody, especially his social superiors, and at times even himself. Bai Ganyu was originally a smart and ruthless peasant.

Keeping pace with the modern world, Bulgarians have wittily transformed Bai Ganyu the peasant into Ganev the aspiring engineer, who shamelessly boasts of Bulgarian achievements in science and technology. He tends to say the wrong things, yet some of his blunders are telling

CUCKOO CLOCKS AND FAX IMPLANTS

At an international fair of new technologies, the Russians exhibited a clock with a little bird that came out on the hour crying loudly, "Lenin! Lenin!" But engineer Ganev got the better of the Russians by exhibiting a very similar clock. Only, instead of the bird, it was a figure of Lenin who came out, crying, "Cuckoo! Cuckoo!"

At a conference of new technologies the American representative bragged that cellular phones and pagers had long been outmoded in the United States. Instead, he said, Americans used a tiny implant in their fingernail to send and receive information.

The Japanese representative claimed that they too had a similar device—but implanted in the tooth. At this point, engineer Ganev burped loudly but was quick to say, "I'm sorry, I just received a fax."

TEN PENNIES AND A CHUCKLE

Here is one of the stories in which Sly Peter scores a point over the chorbadjia, the richest man of the village.

Sly Peter and the chorbadjia were in a public bath. As soon as the chorbadjia finished his bath, he wound a sheet round himself and conceitedly asked, "Peter, seeing me as I am, nearly naked, how much do you estimate I'm worth?"

"Hum," Sly Peter thought for a moment. "You're worth ten Turkish pennies."

"You fool!" The chorbadjia was angry. "Why, the sheet alone costs ten Turkish pennies!"

"I know," Sly Peter said calmly. "That's why I said ten Turkish pennies."

comments on his international competitors. The first of the tales on these pages dates from Bulgaria's Communist era, and the second is typical of Bulgarian humor today.

Young people such as this group of weekend berry-pickers are as adept as their elders at telling Sly Peter or Bai Ganyu jokes.

FESTIVALS

BULGARIAN FESTIVALS ARE VARIED and lively. Some are Christian holidays, some have pagan origins, and some commemorate historical events in Bulgaria. They can involve indoor activities, where families and close friends gather together to feast and chat, or they may be celebrated outdoors, in the city squares, in schoolyards, vineyards, or by the seaside and river banks. Some have fixed dates, some are moveable feasts, while others go on for longer than a day.

Opposite: **Men with huge masks and cowbells around their waists are a distinctive sight at carnival time.**

WHEN IT IS TIME TO CELEBRATE

National Holidays

Mar 3	The Liberation of Bulgaria (regaining of national independence from the Ottoman empire)
May 1	Labor Day
May 24	Day of Letters (Day of Bulgarian education and culture, of the Slav letters, and the Bulgarian Press)

Winter Holidays

Dec 25–27	Christmas
Jan 1	Vassilyovden (St. Vassil's Day)
Jan 6	Yordanovden (Epiphany)
Jan 7	Ivanovden (St. John the Baptist's Day)
Jan 18	Atanasovden (St. Athanasius' Day)

Pre-Spring Holidays

Feb 14	Trifon Zarezan (Day of the Vineyards)
Feb	(specific Sunday) Zagovezni (Shrovetide)
Mar 1	Baba Marta
March	(specific Saturday) Todorovden (St. Todor's Day)

Spring Holidays

April	(specific Sunday) Easter
May 6	Gergyovden (St. George's Day)
May 21	St. Constantine and St. Helena

Fall Holidays

Oct 26	Dimitrovden (St. Dimitri's Day)
Nov	Day of the Souls

THE WANDERING NATIONAL HOLIDAY

Until the "gentle revolution" of 1989, the Bulgarian national holiday was celebrated on September 9. On this day in 1944, eight months before the end of World War II in Europe, the Soviet army reached the capital Sofia in their advance toward Berlin. An anti-fascist alliance of political forces, called the Fatherland Front, came to power, but it was in turn completely taken over by the Communist Party less than three years later.

September 9, 1944 thus became the first day of Bulgaria's Socialist era. This day used to be celebrated in the grandiose style of Communist governments—with students and employees parading en masse in front of red-clad tribunes, and with Communist Party dignitaries enjoying the cheers of the people.

After the collapse of Communism, Bulgarians recognized the need for a national holiday that would mean much more than the triumph of some political power. The new date picked for a national holiday was March 3, the day of the signing of the San Stefano peace treaty after the Russian-

Turkish Liberation War of 1877–1878. This treaty reestablished the Bulgarian state after five centuries of Ottoman rule. March 3 symbolized the day when Bulgaria's dreams of national liberty and unity came true, if only briefly.

UNTIL THE STORK COMES

One of the most cheerful Bulgarian holidays is the day of Baba Marta, on March 1. The name derives from the month of March. According to the Bulgarians, March is a "female month," since its weather changes as fast as the mood of "old Grandma Marta."

Early on the morning of Barba Marta day, Bulgarians tie little red and white tassels on each other, or pin them on their coats with a wish for health, vigor, and happiness. These red-and-white decorations are called *martenitzi* ("mahr-tay-NI-tzi"). In the countryside, people tie these tassels on domestic animals and fruit trees. The red and the white colors symbolize the blood of the new life that is awakening in the snow-covered country.

Children and adults wear the *martenitzi* in anticipation of spring, said to arrive with the storks from the south. When the first stork is sighted, Bulgarians take off their tassels and tie them onto a blossoming tree.

The older women enjoy dressing up for folk festivals.

Schoolchildren in a Day of Letters parade, which celebrates education and culture, the invention of the Slav alphabet, and the founding of the Bulgarian Press.

LOVE OF LEARNING

In an old tradition, Bulgarians celebrate May 24 as the Day of Letters. This holiday was created back in the days of Ottoman rule by the initiative of an ordinary teacher and embraced with joy and pride by schoolchildren and their parents. Many of the parents—seafarers, artisans, or peasants— were illiterate, but harbored the dream of seeing their children educated and making a better life for themselves.

The Day of Letters is an exciting holiday for all, particularly for children who have just learned to read and write. On this day, the entire Bulgarian nation pays homage and expresses love and gratitude to the apostles of the Slavs, Cyril and Methodius; to their disciples who founded the first schools in Bulgaria; and to the teachers, educators, writers, journalists, actors, musicians, and artists of modern Bulgaria. Schoolchildren bring flowers to their teachers and weave wreaths of ivy and flowers around the portraits of Cyril and Methodius.

CHRISTIAN AND PAGAN RITES

Festivals observed during the year include Christmas and the January winter festivals, spring festivals, Easter, harvest holidays, and the Day of the Souls. Christian meaning is often interwoven with ancient pagan rites.

The Christmas holidays go on for 12 days. They begin with *Ignazhden* ("ig-NAHZH-dayn") on December 20 when, according to Bulgarian folklore, Mary felt her first birth pangs. On Christmas Eve, the last day of the Orthodox fast, Bulgarian families gather around the table for the last vegetarian and non-dairy meal of the season. The Orthodox Christmas lasts three days, from December 24 to 26, and religious rituals are supplemented by carnival-like folk festivities. In the evenings, groups of young men go from house to house, singing Christmas songs and blessing the hosts.

A similar tradition, called *survaki* ("SOOR-vah-ki"), is observed on the morning of New Year's Day when children visit their extended family and close friends and neighbors to wish them health and prosperity. They playfully "beat" the elders on the back with a dogwood branch that has been tied with a handkerchief and decorations such as dried plums and popcorn. In return, the youngsters receive fruit, candy, and money.

The dogwood *survachka* ("soor-VAHCH-kah") is chosen for its sturdiness, and because it is the first tree to blossom in the spring.

Buying flowers is a must on a festive day such as the Day of Letters.

A performer with his mask off. Festive gear is eye-catching but can be heavy.

FESTIVAL OF THE VINEYARDS

Holidays in February and March anticipate the regeneration of new life in the spring. Although most of them conform to the Christian Orthodox calendar, they have the distinct flavor of pagan times. On *Trifon Zarezan* ("TRI-fon zah-ray-ZAHN"), the festival of the vineyards, the vines are trimmed in a mood of cheerful celebrations and wine-drinking. Cleansing rituals that are supposed to banish evil powers mark *Zagovezni* ("zah-go-vayz-NI").

This is carnival time in some parts of the country. Men put on festive clothes, huge elaborate masks, and cowbells—to dance their way through village streets and chase away evil spirits.

The Easter holidays, preceded by Lent and a three-day strict fast for the most devout Orthodox Christians, culminate in church services and rituals that mark the week of Christ's Passion on the cross and his resurrection. For centuries, Easter has been the most important holiday for the Eastern Orthodox Christians.

One of the most beloved activities of Easter is the dying of hardboiled eggs on the eve of Good Friday. The first egg is always dyed red and is then put under the family icon, where it remains until Easter Sunday. The next egg is dyed green, the color associated with spring and St. George, whose day falls shortly after Easter, on May 6. The eggs are preserved until Easter morning when the whole family gathers around the table for the traditional breakfast of eggs and plaited Easter breads, richly decorated with almonds and raisins.

For sheep breeders or shepherds, St. George's Day is a very special day.

DAY OF THE SHEPHERD AND OTHERS

The springtime holidays, associated with the names of various saints, have a strong undertone of ancient pagan rites. The celebrations are wild and boisterous, and whole villages go out into the fields or the village square to dance. A number of rituals are dedicated to young people and to nature. One of the biggest May holidays is St. George's day, the day of the shepherd. It is a true regional festival in the stockbreeding parts of the country, where people go to the mountains for games and to dance and feast on whole roasted lambs.

In the fall there are harvest festivals and rituals commemorating the dead. The day of St. Dimitar deserves special mention, as it marks the end of the agricultural cycle that begins on St. George's Day. Bulgarians observe Day of the Souls or *Zadushnitza* ("zah-DOOSH-ni-tzah"). They prepare the traditional dish of bloated wheat and some of the favorite cakes and candies of their deceased relatives. Families go to the cemeteries, where they place flowers on the graves of their loved ones and distribute the prepared food.

FOOD

A LOVE OF GOOD FOOD brings people together in this largely introvert culture. Families make sure they have at least one daily meal together. They would rather have a late dinner than exclude a family member who has been stuck in traffic, or is late returning from work or school.

Sunday lunches are usually small family feasts, complete with wine and elaborate desserts. Bulgarians, both men and women, love to cook, eat, and talk about food.

There is food at any important occasion, whether it is a party, a celebration, or a commemoration of the dead. Even casual visitors to a Bulgarian house will be given something to eat; if they are house guests, they will get three excellent meals a day.

Opposite: **An entire roast lamb is being prepared for a feast on St. George's day.**

Below: **A honey stall in a market in Sofia. Bulgarians love desserts with honey.**

EATING AND DRINKING MANNERS

Lunch is traditionally the biggest meal of the day. It includes some kind of vegetable or meat soup, the main course (often with a small salad on the side), and dessert. It is usually washed down with a glass of wine, which may be diluted with soda water. Teenage children are allowed to have a glass of light wine with their meals. Bulgarians, who are not heavy drinkers, do not see any harm in this. They believe that if their children are taught to drink in moderation during a good meal, they are unlikely to end up as victims of alcohol abuse.

Favorite nonalcoholic drinks include various nectars, fruit juices, and diluted yogurt. Desserts tend to be sweetmeats in rich sugar or honey syrup, compotes of dried or conserved fruit, or puddings.

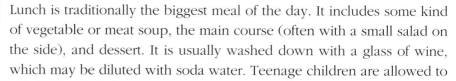

A man buys a sandwich from a city cafeteria. As a rule, Bulgarians try to make their lunch more of an occasion.

BREAKFAST AND SUPPER Breakfast is usually a hurried affair. Everyone in the house will simply grab a cup of tea or coffee and a piece of toast, and dash out of the house. Leisurely breakfasts are reserved for the weekend, when pancakes may be on the table, or a warm cheese-and-egg pastry, or French toast with honey.

Bulgarian suppers are true rituals in relaxation. Lighter than lunch, they start with a fresh salad or an appetizer of pickled vegetables and an aperitif. The most popular aperitifs include *rakiya* ("rah-KI-yah"), the local grape or plum brandy, and *mastika* ("mahs-TI-kah"), an aniseed-based brandy. They are sipped slowly, slightly chilled. The main course tends to be a meat dish, followed by a light dessert, usually fruit or a compote.

A couple prepares winter pickles in their kitchen.

COMPLIMENTS TO THE COOK

Bulgarians make a habit of placing all cutlery, condiments, and food on the table at the beginning of the meal. Once everyone is seated, nobody wants to be interrupted; in fact it is considered impolite to interrupt the meal to ask for something.

Wolfing down one's food without commenting on its taste is also considered rude. People are expected to keep up an easy conversation at mealtimes and to leave nothing uneaten on their plate. Asking for an extra serving is much appreciated and regarded as a compliment to the cook. In the afternoon a good lunch is often followed by a nap.

Bulgarians are meticulous about the use of a knife and fork. But they sometimes eat fish or chicken with their fingers. Except when eating pasta, they rarely spread a napkin across their laps. Only children do that, but adults are expected to eat tidily. Napkins are used to wipe one's mouth at the end of each course, or before taking a drink.

Young hikers in the Pirin mountains share a meal of cheese and bread.

MEALS FOR ALL SEASONS

Bulgarian cooking uses seasonal ingredients to their full potential. Meat consumption, especially of pork and poultry, goes up substantially in the winter months. Stews and hearty soups, using all parts of the animal or bird, are common dishes. Sizzling pork chops or pork stews with canned vegetable sauces or sauerkraut are favorites, with an accompanying bottle or two of wine.

A favorite aperitif in the cold winter months is *greyana rakiya* ("GRAY-an-nah rah-KI-yah"), a plum or grape brandy heated with honey in a copper pot and served in tiny thick cups.

Spring is the time to enjoy lamb with the first green vegetables—dock, spinach, and green onions. The summer diet is lighter and mostly vegetarian, using lots of fresh fruit and vegetables.

Yogurt makes its appearance at almost every meal. It is usually made from cow's milk, but yogurt from sheep's milk is a much sought-after delicacy. From the age of three months onward, most Bulgarians have yogurt every day. But the Western practice of mixing yogurt with fruit and nuts is uncommon.

Certain seasonal foods are available only briefly. These include lamb and most fruits and vegetables. A shepherd's specialty from the Rhodope mountains called *kotmach* ("kot-MAHCH") deserves special mention. It is made from sheep's milk—but only in the month of August when grazing pastures have dried out and the sheep are nearing the end of their lactation period, so that their milk is at its densest and considered suitable.

LIVE BIRDS AND FRUIT FROM THE MARKET

Markets in the cities are open all year round, but the most fascinating time to shop at these lively outdoor markets is in the fall, and especially on Saturdays. Stallholders come to sell their fresh produce in the cities, sometimes from as far away as 200 miles (320 km).

All manner of goods and produce can be found at the market—live birds, lamb in season, fresh fruit and vegetables, honey, fish, flowers, and nuts, as well as handicrafts, homespun woolen yarn, or handknit sweaters.

The market day starts at seven in the morning, and by six in the evening most stallholders are packing up and ready to go. Bulgarians are not accustomed to haggling, and the only time they might get a real bargain is in the late afternoon—when vendors are in a hurry to go home and willing to negotiate.

Bulgarians eat a lot of bread. A family of four goes through a two-pound loaf or more within a day. They like their bread fresh and buy it daily. Bread is rarely baked at home, except for the New Year pita bread or the pleated Easter breads baked in traditional homes. Popular all year round is a slice of warm, heavy, crusty bread topped with feta cheese and slices of tomato.

SARMI WITH CABBAGE LEAVES

This is a recipe for 5–6 servings.

1 small head of cabbage	$^1/_2$ cup rice
salt and 2 tablespoons vinegar	2 eggs, beaten
$^1/_2$ lb (500 g) veal	parsley
$^1/_2$ lb (500 g) fat pork or mutton	paprika, black pepper, and salt to taste
1 small cube of lard	1–2 cups beef broth
$^1/_3$ cup vegetable oil	2 tablespoons flour
2 medium onions, finely chopped	$^1/_2$ cup yogurt

Choose 12–13 perfect cabbage leaves and trim the big veins. Put in a shallow pan, cover with boiling water, add salt and vinegar and let stand for 5–6 minutes. Grind meat together or chop finely and mix. Heat the lard and 2–3 tablespoons of oil and sauté the finely chopped onions. Add meat and stir until browned. Set aside. Mix together with rice, eggs, parsley, paprika, black pepper, and salt to taste.

Divide the mixture evenly among the cabbage leaves and wrap each leaf tightly around the filling to make the sarmi. In the bottom of a large shallow pot place several layers of cabbage leaves, and then put the sarmi in tight layers into the pot. Cover with boiling broth and drizzle with the rest of the heated oil. Put a plate on top to press down.

Bring to a boil, then lower the heat and let simmer for 40–60 minutes. Shake the pot once in a while and add a little more broth, if necessary.

To prepare the yogurt sauce, brown the flour in a little oil, add broth and yogurt, and season with salt and lemon zest. Spoon on top of the sarmi.

INFLUENCES AND VARIATIONS

Bulgarian cuisine reflects many different influences. It may be vegetarian or based on dairy products. Regional cuisines may recall Russian or central Asian influences, or the cooking of neighboring Yugoslavia and Romania. In fact, as far as cooking goes, there are likely to be more pronounced differences within the regions of Bulgaria than when crossing state borders in the Balkans.

Traditional cooking in the Rhodope mountains rarely involves frying. This is probably the healthiest regional cooking in the country. It uses very little oil, which is usually added to the food only when it has been cooked for some time. Marinating, grinding, or blanching the cooking ingredients are not typical of this region. Rhodope meals are examples of simple and natural cooking at its best. This style uses a lot of garlic, nuts, and dairy products. The best known specialty from the Rhodope is *cheverme* ("chay-vayr-MAY"), a meal cooked outdoors for big family holidays or for town or village festivals. A whole lamb is roasted on a spit, then served with honey and a seasonal salad.

In the Thracian plain bordering on the Rhodope area, cooking methods closely resemble those in Greece. Vegetables, olive oil, and spices are favorite ingredients. Meals are often cooked in several stages. Meats and vegetables are first prefried, then stewed or baked, and then topped off with a sauce. The dish of vine leaves stuffed with meat and rice known as rolled *lozovi sarmi* ("LO-zo-vi sahr-MI") has a yogurt sauce.

MARINADES AND SEAFOOD

In the plains north of the Balkan range, marinating food is a popular technique. Northern Bulgarian cuisine uses a lot of finely chopped meats. Popular dishes include a layered pastry with rice and meat filling and baked sweet red peppers stuffed with beans.

Residents of the Black Sea coast and those living along the Danube are spoiled for choice when it comes to fresh fish. Bulgarians like their seafood simple—grilled or deep-fried with a touch of lemon. But some holiday recipes do call for baked fish stuffed with finely chopped tomatoes, onions, chili peppers, and nuts.

Fish are plentiful along the Black Sea coast. Fish roe paste is a popular appetizer.

BULGARIA

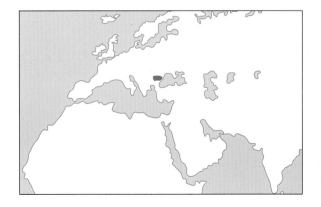

QUICK NOTES

OFFICIAL NAME
People's Republic of Bulgaria

AREA
42,823 square miles (110,912 square kilometers)

POPULATION
8,775,198

POPULATION GROWTH RATE
−0.25%

CAPITAL
Sofia

ADMINISTRATIVE REGIONS
Burgas, Sofia City, Haskovo, Lovech, Montana, Plovdiv, Ruse, Sofia, Varna

FORM OF GOVERNMENT
Parliamentary republic

OFFICIAL LANGUAGE
Bulgarian

NATIONAL ANTHEM
"Mila Rodino" ("Dear Homeland")

NATIONAL FLAG
Three equal horizontal bands of white (top), green, and red

NATIONAL FLOWER
Rose

MAJOR RIVERS
Danube (northern border), Iskar, Maritsa

MAJOR RELIGION
Bulgarian Orthodox

HIGHEST POINT
Mount Musala, 9,596 feet (2,924 meters)

COASTLINE
175 miles (282 kilometers)

CURRENCY
Lev (widely fluctuating exchange rate, most recently US$1 = 67 leva)

NATURAL RESOURCES
Copper, lead, zinc, coal, timber, arable land

MAIN EXPORTS
Machinery and equipment, foodstuffs, including wine and tobacco, manufactured consumer goods, fuels, nonferrous metals, iron, steel

LEADERS IN POLITICS
Boris III, Tzar of Bulgaria (1919–1943);
Alexander Stamboliyski, Prime Minister (1919–1923);
Georgi Dimitrov, Prime Minister (1946–1949);
Todor Zhivkov, Prime Minister (1962–1971), Chairman of the State Council (1971–1989)
Zhelyu Zhelev, President (since 1990)
Zhan Videnov, Prime Minister (since 1995)
Ivan Kostov, leader of the Union of Democratic Forces

GLOSSARY

Bogomils ("BOH-goh-mils")
Members of the medieval Bulgarian sect holding that God is the father of two sons, Jesus the Savior and Satan the creator of the material world.

boyar ("BOH-yahr")
A Bulgarian feudal lord.

Bulgars ("BOOL-gahrs")
A nomadic tribe of Turanian origin, which formed a coalition with the Balkan Slavs and founded the Bulgarian state in A.D. 681.

chorbadjiya ("chor-BAHD-ji-ya")
The richest Bulgarian in a village of the last century, often a collaborator of the local Turkish government.

Cyrillic ("ser-IL-lik")
The alphabet created by Cyril and Methodius and used for the writing of the Slavic languages.

Day of Letters
An important national holiday on May 24, when the Bulgarian nation celebrates education and learning and pays homage to scholars of the past and present.

glasnost ("GLAHZ-nost")
Literally, "openness." The declared public policy of openly and frankly discussing economic and political realities, first introduced in the former Soviet Union in 1985.

haidouk ("hai-DOOK")
Member of the spontaneous underground movement against the Ottoman government that started in the last decade of the 14th century.

horo ("ho-RO")
A circular folk dance of a number of the Balkan peoples.

Ignazhden ("ig-NAHZH-dayn")
A festival on December 20 marking the first day of the Christmas holidays.

Nestinar ("nays-ti-NAH")
A person with the gift of dancing on red-hot embers on May 21, the day of the saints Contantine and Helena.

patriarch ("PAY-tri-ark")
The head of the Bulgarian church.

perestroika ("pay-re-STROY-kah")
Literally, "reformation." The transformation of the Communist economic and political system into a free-market democracy.

rakiya ("rah-KI-yah")
A Bulgarian grape or plum brandy popular as an aperitif.

survaki ("SOOR-vah-ki")
A tradition observed on New Year's Day, when children visit their elders and family friends to wish them health and prosperity.

BIBLIOGRAPHY

The Devil's Dozen: Thirteen Bulgarian Women Poets. Tr. Brenda Walker with Belin Tonchev. Boston: Forest Books, 1990.

"History's Cauldron." *Atlantic Monthly* 267:6 (June 1991), 93-96.

Kaplan, Robert. "Bulgaria: Tales from Communist Byzantium." Part 3 of *Balkan Ghosts: A Journey Through History*, 193-230. New York: St. Martin's Press, 1993.

Resnick, Abraham. *Enchantment of the World: Bulgaria.* Chicago: Children's Press, 1995.

Young Poets of New Bulgaria: An Anthology. Ed. Belin Tonchev. Boston: Forest Books, 1990.

INDEX

INDEX

dance, 87, 88, 89
Day of Letters, 107, 110
Day of the Shepherd, 113
Day of the Souls, 107, 113
demonstrations, 28–29, 33, 39
desserts, 115, 116
Dimitrova, Blaga, 34
drama, 15, 95
dress, 55, 109
drinks, 116, 118

Easter, 107, 111, 112–113, 119
Ecoglasnost, 29
economic reforms, 37
education, 19, 23, 54, 64–65, 69, 73, 84, 107, 110
elections, 28, 29, 31, 32, 33, 34, 35
environmental issues, 39
excavations, archeological, 94–95
exports, 10, 37, 40, 41

family, 58, 60, 61, 62, 63, 66, 100, 113, 115
fauna, 12, 13
First Bulgarian Kingdom, 17, 19
flora, 13
  rose, 8, 13
fruit, 40, 116, 118, 119

gardening, 66, 98
Germany, 27, 32, 51, 54
Grandmother's Day, 59
Greece, 7, 26, 51, 53, 69, 121
Greeks, 17, 26, 45, 47, 50, 53, 79, 87
Gypsies, 26, 45, 46, 49, 50, 75

handicrafts, 49, 50, 87, 119
holidays, 59, 69, 99, 107–113
humor, 102–105

independence, 24, 107
industry, 8, 9, 10, 12, 14, 15, 26, 37, 38–39, 40, 41, 65

Islam, 22, 49, 53, 62, 76
Ivan Asen II, 21

Jews, 24, 26, 27, 45, 51, 53, 76, 85

Kaloyan, 21
Khan Asparuh, 17
Khan Krum, 18
Konstantinov, Aleko, 104

lakes, 12
land laws, customs, 40–41, 52
languages
  Armenian, 79
  Bulgarian, 19, 23, 46, 79–81
  Greek, 26, 51, 79, 80, 81, 85, 91
  learning, 64
  Macedonian, 26, 79
  Roma, 49
  Slavic, 18, 19, 26, 72–73, 80–81
  Turkish, 48, 49, 53, 79
legal code, 18
Levski, Vassil, 24
literature, 19, 20, 23, 80, 87, 91
livestock, 9, 40

Macedonia, 7, 21, 25, 26, 69, 79
Macedonian Question, 25, 26
markets, 119
Marmara, Sea of, 7
marriage, 57, 60–61, 63, 69, 84, 85
meals, 115, 116, 118, 121
Mediterranean Sea, 7, 11, 43
Methodius, 18, 72, 80, 81, 110
Mladenov, Petar, 31, 33, 34
Moesia, 17, 25
Montenegro, 26
mountains, 7, 11, 101
  Athos, 23, 91
  Balkans, 7, 8, 21, 25
  Pirin, 7, 9
  Rhodope, 9, 49, 101, 118, 120, 121
  Rila, 9, 101

Strandja, 89
Vitosha, 15, 101
music, 15, 49, 87–89
Muslims, 22, 48, 49, 60, 69, 75, 76, 79

names, 49, 53, 84–85
National Revival, 22, 23–24, 26, 64, 73, 90, 91

Ottoman empire/rule, 21, 22, 23, 24, 25, 26, 45, 46, 48, 49, 73, 89, 90, 107, 109, 110

Paisii, Father, 23, 73
Parliament, 32, 33, 34–35, 41
political parties
  Bulgarian Socialist Party (BSP), 29, 31, 32, 33, 35
  Communist Party, 27, 29, 31, 32, 108
  Fatherland Front, 27, 32, 108
  Union of Democratic Forces (UDF), 29, 34, 35
Pomaks, 45, 49, 50, 75
population, 14, 15, 26, 37, 39, 45, 49, 52, 53, 57, 69
proverbs, 47

radio, 35
reading habit, 97, 102
Rhodope, 21, 88
rivers
  Danube, 7, 12, 21, 25, 42, 43, 76, 121
  Maritsa, 15
  Yantra, 8
Romania, 7, 26, 51, 69, 77, 120
Romanians, 19, 45
Romans, Roman empire, 17, 21, 46, 87, 95
Russia, 24, 79, 80, 120
Russians, 19, 24, 45, 104

INDEX